Gardener's Companion Series

The Missouri Gardener's Companion

*An Insider's Guide to
Gardening in the Show-Me State*

Becky Homan

Guilford, Connecticut

To buy books in quantity for corporate use
or incentives, call **(800) 962–0973**
or e-mail **premiums@GlobePequot.com.**

Text design by Casey Shain
Illustrations by Josh Yunger
Maps by M. A. Dubé © Morris Book Publishing, LLC
Map p. 23 (bottom) adapted with permission of the Arbor Day Foundation.

Library of Congress Cataloging-in-Publication Data

Homan, Becky.
  The Missouri gardener's companion : an insider's guide to gardening in the Show-Me state / Becky Homan.
    p. cm.
Includes index.
ISBN 13: 978-0-7627-4652-1
1. Gradening—Missouri. I. Title.
SB453.2.M8H66 2008
635.09778—dc22   2008000051

Manufactured in the United States of America

10 9 8 7 6 5 4 3 2 1

To Dianne O'Connell, a friend and teacher,
and to Cindy Gilberg, a generous person and a pioneer
in Missouri perennial gardening

Contents

Introduction

I moved to Missouri in March 1980, just in time to weather one of the hotter summers on record. I wasn't an active gardener then. I certainly wasn't much of a St. Louisan: I arrived without an air conditioner, an unholy sin considering the frequent blasts of hot, humid air that punish both Missouri people and plants in June, July, and August.

Then came winter—a series of hard freezes followed by mid-winter thaws that cracked ground and exposed tender roots of smaller landscape plants around my apartment building. What, I wondered, can grow in this antagonistic climate? Other Missouri gardening newbies must ask themselves that same question. The answer is, a lot.

Even gardeners with intermediate and advanced skills around the state struggle with issues of soil, climate, and water as well as diseases, pests, and invasive plants. But they also tend fantastic arrays—large and small—of annuals, herbs, vegetables, native plants, perennials, trees, and shrubs as well as the grasses in their pristine lawns. The purpose of this book is to help explain how this is done—roughly in the order mentioned above—in a most basic and stress-free way. Good gardening practices, for instance, can help prevent harm to plants in cases of those quick Missouri shifts from freeze to thaw, or of drought, or of other harsh realities of gardening life in this transitional area between northern plains and southern states.

And if you make an effort to learn, you'll meet some of the fantastic characters who garden around the state. I did. I'd said those two little words—"Road trip!"—when I started work on this book. And four drives across the state later, I'd met master gardeners in Kansas City who spent a gorgeous spring day driving me to a dozen of their top home gardens. I'd hung out with herbalists, hippies, and mostly average folks at the Baker Creek

Heirloom Seed Festival, whose impresario, Jere Gettle, is a twenty-something cowboy from Montana now working farmland and saving heirloom seeds near Springfield. I'd been northwest to Savannah, Missouri, for gorgeous perennials and southeast to Charleston, Missouri, for hybrid azaleas. And I'd found dozens of other niche gardeners around the state, including Jeff Oberhaus and his fantastic tropical plants sold from greenhouses in hill country bordering prairie at Vintage Hill Farm near Franklin. There's Judy Allmon in Jefferson City, who founded the state's innovative Grow Native! program, and Mervin Wallace, whose Missouri Wildflowers Nursery is the gold standard for native plants in the region. Also in Jeff City I'd met the very affable Don Schnieders, a retired excavator, now host of a local gardening radio show who has what's arguably the best vegetable garden in the state.

There are too many other amazing Missouri gardeners to mention here. Suffice it to say that they're everywhere in the book, as owners of independent garden centers, arborists, horti-

culturists, master gardeners, amateur gardeners, rain-garden experts, and organic-gardening fans. Ones from east-central Missouri are especially important to me from my reporting days as garden editor at the *St. Louis Post-Dispatch*. And I've learned a lot over the years from a personal connection—the amateur gardener who's also my husband, Alex Shaffer. We met in St. Louis. He's a biologist and a New Orleans native. When we'd visit his hometown in the mid-1980s and early '90s, we'd not only see the marvels of Mardi Gras and great restaurants of the Crescent City but also the Garden District and his family's Uptown neighborhood. We'd make mental notes of many small, charming landscapes and bring ideas home to brighten our old, two-story house. We still have thick borders of the variegated liriope that came north from a first trip. We keep another variegated New Orleans find—a huge tropical bougainvillea—alive on a south-facing kitchen windowsill. It must be twenty years old, with fuchsia blooms in late winter. And a half-dozen orchids that lived permanently on the in-laws' back fence now grace our Missouri fence in summer, getting through the winters indoors, under fluorescent lights.

If truth be told, however, it was a single St. Louis Master Gardener, Alma Reitz, who had the biggest impact on me. Alex and I had met her at a Missouri Botanical Garden plant sale in the early eighties. "Do you sell ferns here?" we asked her. "No," she replied, and paused, "but if you want ferns, bring a bucket of good dirt to my house tomorrow morning." And she scribbled down her address. We showed up. She told us where to dig up dozens of ostrich ferns and how to fill in holes with our soil. The ferns made more. We now give them away every year. Alma later gave me other great, no-nonsense advice. She encouraged me to try for a St. Louis Master Gardener slot. And she backed my campaign to get bosses at the *Post-Dispatch* to create a full-time garden-editor position. They did. It all worked out well for me, for the newspaper, and, most important, for readers.

In early retirement I garden quite differently. I tweak perennials here, add annuals there, in my tiny city backyard. Mostly I help my mother, Marilyn Homan, keep up with the grounds of her vintage 1920s condominium. I get asked to help friends with their garden designs, although I'm much more of a writer and photographer than I am a great gardener. When I can, I get help, too—especially for this book. It comes from a buddy, MaryAnn Fink, now coordinator of the Missouri Landscape and Nursery Association; from a wealth of top-notch Missouri independent garden centers; and from such gurus as June Hutson and Chip Tynan, both senior horticulturists at the Missouri Botanical Garden, and Alan Branhagen, horticulture director at Powell Gardens near Kansas City.

But occasionally, when my own yard starts to overgrow with plants—most of them healthy, a few faltering—I think back to what Alma Reitz told me early on. "Be ruthless," she said. And so I selectively tear out, find good homes for most plants, toss marginal ones in the yard-waste Dumpster, and move on.

Firm Foundations

Soils

There may be no better place to think about gardening than in Missouri. It is a state that's located at the heart of the nation, with currents, trends, and themes coming at it from all directions. And its soils—the heart of any good garden—are about as diverse as cold winds roaring across Missouri from the northern plains are from warm, humid drafts of air coming up from below the state's southern border.

"We're basically at the crossroads of the country with our soils, just like with anything else," says Missouri State Soil Scientist Dennis Potter. "And for a Midwest state, soils here are more diverse than most."

Indeed, the state's range of soil material is so vast that some counties report as many as fifty different soil types, each named after area landmarks or towns. But generally, says Potter, they are "prairie soils from the north and west, Ozark soils coming in from Arkansas, and alluvial soils from the Mississippi River valley." Loess, as certain windblown soils are called, also figures in and is "a fairly unique phenomenon in this state," says Potter.

So what's a good gardener to do? Take a painless minicourse in soils, that's what, to determine what you're growing in. Soil knowledge and improvement are the two most important aspects of any gardening scheme. They're arguably more important than the plants you put into the ground. Knowing what your soils are—heavy, as with Missouri's ubiquitous clays—is especially important so that you can make them more open and free draining, as well as moisture retentive while also kept in just the right acid or alkaline range. Improvements make for a balanced growing medium that ultimately anchors plants in an underground network where correct levels of moisture and nutrients get to the roots. And happy roots make for happy plants, as the old garden saying goes. With great soil even a Missouri brown thumb may turn the landscape a bright and healthy green.

What Is Soil?

Stated most simply, soil is the top layer of the earth's surface. Its basis is found in three important mineral particles—sand, clay, and silt. When a combination of sand, clay, and silt combine with water, air, decaying plants, and other organic matter, you've got the makings of a good growing medium—one that holds on to nutrients and to just enough water so that air still is available to roots.

Sand we all know about. Fine grains of the stuff stick to wet feet on our summer vacations and find their way into just about every item of beach gear. But there is sand in landlocked Missouri, too. Most grains of it in this state contain quartz. Very fine sand particles may be as small as 0.05 millimeter or, say, one-twentieth the size of a grain of salt, while very coarse sand may be forty times larger, at 2 millimeters in diameter. A sandy soil is defined by Missouri state and U.S. Department of Agriculture soil surveys as one with 85 percent or more sand and not more than 10 percent clay. Sandy soils do not hold on to nutrients well; rains and irrigation tend to wash right through this growing medium.

Clay, surprisingly enough, has the finest mineral particles of all—each less than 0.002 millimeter in size. Ions of electricity actually weld these tiny bits of clay together into what can be an impenetrable mass. We think of clay for pots as the dense, sticky, wet material that can be pressed into a lump for spinning on a potter's wheel. A clay soil, generally, is one that has 40 percent or more of these finest mineral bits plus, perhaps, equal parts sand and silt.

It's not a death sentence in gardening to inherit clay soils. In fact, clays also have negative electric charges that help the soil hold on to such positively charged nutritional elements as potassium, calcium, and magnesium. Therefore, clay can be a very fertile soil. But its dense structure means that it drains poorly. For home gardens, clay soil needs to be lightened with compost and other organic amendments that help to physically separate dense clay bits from one another.

Silt sits right in the middle of any soils chart. Silt has a floury feel, with mineral particles that range in diameter from the upper limit of clay to the lower limit of very fine sand. A silty soil, as defined by soil surveys, consists of 80 percent or more of silt and less than 12 percent clay.

And the best gardening soils from all of these? A combo platter of sand, clay, and silt is the answer. It's often called loam. Loamy soils will not feel sticky in your hand. They hold plenty of moisture but also drain well enough so that air reaches the roots.

Personally, says soil scientist Potter, he likes a soil with "silt loam or loam textures, with about 50 percent silt, 25 percent

Quick Soil Identifier

Pick up a small amount of moist—not wet—soil from your garden and rub it between your fingers. If it feels gritty and doesn't stick together, it's sandy. A sandy loam, on the other hand, will have a bit more cohesion. If your soil feels soft and floury to the touch, it's more likely to be silt. Silt loam, too, may hold together a bit better. And clay is the most cohesive of all—forming a sticky ball when you first squeeze it in the palm of your hand and then rolling into a ribbon as you work it with your fingers. If your soil is more of a clay loam, it also holds together but works into a thinner, less sticky ribbon.

sand, and 25 percent clay." But whatever the ratio, he likes mixing in lots of organic matter—as much as 3 inches of peat, compost, or very well-rotted manure. He layers this on top of the soil before starting a new garden bed and mixes it at least a half foot deep into the earth.

What Is in Your Missouri Soil?

Think of a disaster movie—circa 500,000 years ago. In it, massive glaciers from a last ice age pummel the earth's surface in a slow slide south across what is now the Iowa border. They literally grind to a halt where the Missouri River now bisects the state from west to east. Glaciers leave heaps of till—or earth plus large rock fragments up to boulder size—on the surface and underneath.

These pummeled soils to the north of the Missouri River have settled onto rock-filled, gently to steeply sloping areas or onto prairies or rich bottom lands. Those soils to the south of the river formed very differently. They were not created by moving glaciers but developed as bedrock, plants, and animals decomposed in place over eons.

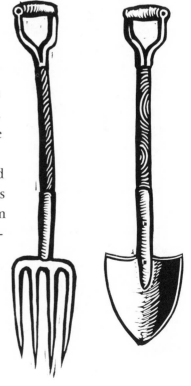

Both sides of the river benefited from a wind that lifted silt deposits from melting ice and carried them across much of the state. That wind-blown soil is called loess. It is thickest on the bluffs along the Missouri River and gradually becomes thinner with distance from the river valley.

Other original, or "parent," soils besides loess include the river-deposited alluvium and the residuum soil that—as the name implies—"resided" in Missouri for eons and eroded or decomposed in place. You'll need to concern yourself mostly with offspring of these parents. It's the offspring that show up in your yard or garden and ultimately create a good, or challenging, place for plants to grow. But for the sake of understanding how diverse soils are in Missouri, let's take a look at just a few offspring in a sampling of soils from three counties around the state.

Jackson County, home to much of Kansas City, has a significant number of soils that developed under this western Missouri county's mostly treeless, tallgrass prairie. Today only scattered pockets of prairie remain. Some of the county's soils are found under structures and parking lots—so-called Urban Land soil types. However, many soils in Jackson County bear the names of local landmarks, such as Sibley, Sharpsburg, and Macksburg silt loams, and have moderate to high amounts of organic matter, according to state soil surveys. These, and alluvial (river deposited) soils, make for excellent home gardens, as long as flooding isn't an issue. Jackson County is located just south of the Missouri River and includes areas of wide floodplains.

Howard County is smack in the middle of the state, just north of the Missouri River in what scientists call the Central Mississippi Valley Wooded Slopes area. It is mainly an old glacial-till plain that's been eroded into narrow ridgetops and steeply sloping valley sides. Thick deposits of loess cover the areas closest to the Missouri River, gradually thinning to the east and north. In the northwestern part of the county, small areas of flat prairie soils occupy remnants of the old broad ridgetops. These latter areas are important locally for farming and for the silty loam that makes for excellent home gardening.

St. Louis County is home to the city of St. Louis as well as to a vast array of soils—some good for gardening, others difficult, especially where construction has compacted or completely

Survey Savvy

Getting your county's soil survey is just one way to start improving your own little patch of ground. But it's an interesting place to start—with lots of county history mixed into each survey's text. A survey's documented soil origins often have a direct relationship to the finished product—the tilth, or that fine, crumbly surface layer of soil produced by your own cultivation. Here's where to get soil-survey information for your county:

• Write or call your request to the Office of the State Soil Scientist at Missouri Natural Resources Conservation Service, Parkade Center, 601 Business Loop 70 West, Suite 250, Columbia, MO 65203; (573) 876-0907. Paper survey booklets are free. You may also request a CD of a survey.

• Go online for the most current information on Missouri soils, county by county, at http://websoilsurvey.nrcs .usda.gov/app. And while online, look at a description of the State Soil of Missouri—a silty loam named Menfro that's found on some 780,000 acres of the state, including Hannibal and the home of Mark Twain, St. Charles and land where the first state capitol was built, and Daniel Boone's home near Defiance. Find this in a list of all state soils at http://soils.usda.gov/gallery/state _soils.

• Ask for a new, colorful pamphlet called *From the Ground Down*, a free, new introduction to Missouri soil surveys, available from the address or phone number above.

removed topsoils. Originally covered by an eastern Missouri oak-hickory hardwood forest, this county received more than its share of windblown loess from floodplains of the Missouri River (its northern boundary), Meramec River (to the south), and Mississippi River (to the east). Important to the county today are the deep, well-drained soils that were formed in loess and now are silt loams intermixed through the central corridor of the county with Urban Land soils. But also found along the floodplain of the Missouri River are poorly draining silty and clayey soils, mixed occasionally with soils that are just the opposite—sandy and excessively draining. Major flooding, as recent as 1993 and as distant as prehistory, deposited this alluvial material.

Beyond Soil Surveys: What's in Your Own Backyard?

Take a hint from that old Chicago maxim—vote early and often—and get a soil test early in your gardening career and get more tests "often," as in every three or four years. That's according to James Quinn, a Columbia gardener who also is regional horticulture specialist in seven central Missouri counties for the University of Missouri Extension. Each test reveals soil type, texture, and acidity level, plus how easily the soil drains, which in turn determine what plants will grow there and how easy or hard the soil will be to work.

Many Missourians don't check their soil regularly, says Quinn. "I would advise people that repeated soil testing is probably the correct thing to do," if they want to maintain a nice-looking garden, he says. That's because you're always going to be fighting to restore elements that have been stripped away by rain, wind, and removal of plant material.

Why don't gardeners test their soil? Time and cost, he says, are often mentioned as issues. They shouldn't be. Sampling in the home garden takes no more than a half hour. And every county boasts a relatively convenient extension office (two in the greater Kansas City area and two in St. Louis; see "Where to . . . get forms and take soil samples" on the next page. Soil tests in these urban settings are crucial, Quinn adds, because where new construction's taken place, "a lot of topsoil is stripped away." The soil-test cost, meanwhile, is a moderate $15 to $20, depending on the county.

And consider this: If you have a yard tied up mostly in lawn, get the soils underneath grass tested *separately* from those in which you're growing annuals, vegetables, and/or perennials. It's very likely that you'll have different fertilizer needs for these two gardening situations, as Quinn did. In his own yard he has soil that's heavy and poorly drained, with a substantial amount of clay. To improve drainage and texture, he's focused on increasing the organic matter, especially in raised areas for annual flowers and vegetables and for the roses where "the soil seemed especially sticky," he says. Recent testing showed that nutrient levels are high, which means he doesn't need to spend money on more fertilizer now. His latest tests also showed that perennials—planted in newly purchased topsoil—needed a bit of lime, while some nitrogen was suggested for his lawn. But these were all the amendments his soil required.

Besides saving money on potassium, phosphorus, calcium, and other nutrients, Quinn also felt a bit like he was saving the earth. "Water quality emanating from urban landscapes is degraded when fertilizers are overapplied," he says. Nitrogen and phosphorus, he adds, are the "nutrients of most concern" for running off in heavy rains and polluting waterways or wells. (See chapter 3, "Water," for some solutions to runoff problems.)

Why pH Is Important

Put simply, pH is a measure of the oh-so-important range of acidity versus alkalinity in soils. The degree of this acidity or alkalinity is expressed as a number between 1 and 14. Soils with a pH of

When to . . . *test soil*

Any time of year that the ground is not frozen. But the off-season of late winter and early spring are especially good times because soil labs aren't as busy with testing as they are when the frenzied season of full-blown spring comes along. And getting results back early gives you a month or two to plan ways to amend your soils with just the right nutrients when spring finally comes. Final thought: Don't be afraid to take your test results to a trusted nursery or garden center; they get these kinds of questions all the time.

How to . . . collect soil samples

Sample the part of the soil where roots grow. That means taking a sample from the surface down about 6 to 9 inches for most annual and perennial beds. Use a clean garden spade or trowel and take a total of about two cups of soil from several different locations in vegetable, annual, and perennial beds, and the same amount from several locations in lawn. Combine the flower- and vegetable-bed soils and let them air-dry on a porch, patio, or deck. Do the same, separately, with lawn soils. Then place each in a clean plastic bag, marked with what you plan to plant (vegetables versus lawn, for instance) and your name and address, and take them to the closest extension-service office for sending off to one of two University of Missouri soil-testing labs in the state. Results are returned to you in the mail in about two weeks. For more how-to information, go to http://soilplantlab.missouri.edu/soil.

Where to . . . get forms and take soil samples

- You may download a soil-test information form at http://extension.missouri.edu/explorepdf/miscpubs/mp0555.pdf.

- Forms are found at your county extension office, where you also deliver your soil sample. For an office near you, call MU Extension at (573) 882-6385 or go online to http://extension.missouri.edu/regions, find your county, click Go and find the Office Staff and Locations.

- In the Kansas City area, for instance, there are two extension offices, at 2700 East Eighteenth Street, Suite 240, Kansas City 64127 (816-482-5850); and in Blue Springs at 1501 NW Jefferson, Suite 110, Blue Springs 64015 (816-252-5051). The Web site is http://extension.missouri.edu/jackson/homegarden.shtml.

- The extension office accepting soil samples in the St. Louis area is at 121 South Meramec, Suite 501, Clayton 63105 (314-615-2911). The Web address is http://extension.missouri.edu/stlouis/location.shtml. Also in the St. Louis area, the Kemper Center for Home Gardening of the Missouri Botanical Garden, 4344 Shaw Boulevard, accepts soil samples to send off to testing labs. Soil sample forms are there as well. Call (314) 577-9440 for more information.

Sweet and Sour?

So-called "sweet soil" is an old-fashioned term used to denote soil that is limy or alkaline. "Sour soil" is an old-fashioned term used to describe exceedingly acid soil, which sometimes has a sour smell. Legend has it that before science developed soil tests, some farmers learned to judge pH by the sniff test. A few others even tasted soil for this purpose. It's legend, after all—meaning don't try this at home.

less than 7 are acid, good for such so-called acid-loving plants as blueberries, strawberries, azaleas, and rhododendrons. Soils with a pH greater than 7 are alkaline.

To put these all in context, pure water is neutral, bringing its pH in at 7. And very generally speaking, a slightly acidic to neutral pH for your soils—somewhere between 6 and 7—is where most plants are able to take up nutrients or, to put it scientifically, have nutrients "made available" to them. If the pH is too low or too high, some nutrients won't dissolve in the water that's also in soil, and therefore those nutrients can't be taken up by plant roots. It's said that many nourishing minerals are held by soil particles and unavailable to plants at incorrect pH levels.

You don't want your nutrients "locked up." Free them. Grow strong and healthy plants. Have your soil tested (see the previous section) to keep the proper pH. Soil pH, by the way, affects the work of certain soil organisms because soils that are too acid slow down the decomposition of organic matter by beneficial bacteria.

And don't err on the opposite end of the pH spectrum, either. "One big mistake a lot of people make is that they put on lime when they don't need to," says soils specialist James Quinn, who reviews some five hundred soil tests in central Missouri each year. "They raise the pH up too high. You cannot believe how over-limed some soils are." Lime is helpful, he adds, "particularly in the Columbia area, where a number of soils have a low pH." And it is only natural to assume that you should keep adding lime when you hear about the lack of it in local soils. But it's possible to add too much. Again, not only is a soil test important, but so is the act of following the written advice provided on the test-result forms from specialists who work with soils every day.

Nutrients Needed to Grow Good Gardens

The nutritious elements that are needed in soil to feed and keep plants going are carbon, hydrogen, and oxygen, available from air and water; nitrogen (N), phosphorus (P), potassium (K), plus calcium, magnesium, and sulfur, all used in relatively large amounts and called macronutrients; and vitamin-like essential trace elements, called micronutrients, including iron, boron, and zinc.

The majors first. Chief among the macronutrients is nitrogen (N). You've seen it mentioned as the first letter in N-P-K references on many garden products, including fertilizers. Nitrogen (N) is essential for vigorous vegetative growth and glossy green leaves. It may be found naturally in the soil in adequate amounts, especially where lots of decomposed organic matter is present. When it's not found, plants look stunted. When there's too much, you have too much growth of soft tissue that's vulnerable to disease or even to damage in an unexpected cold snap. Phosphorus (P), on the other hand, is essential for developing strong, healthy root systems, while potassium (K) improves stem growth and disease-fighting abilities.

The minors next. The micronutrients of iron, chlorine, manganese, zinc, copper, boron, molybdenum, and chlorine are needed in the soil, in small amounts, to round out the supplements. The lack of iron is one of the more common problems associated with chlorosis—a yellowing of leaf tissue. Manganese or zinc deficiencies may also cause leaf yellowing.

Ask a Missouri home-gardening expert, such as June Hutson, about the best sources of these major and minor nutrients, and she'll veer away from the synthetic chemical solutions to give you a different three-word answer: "Compost, compost, compost."

Hutson is a senior horticulturist and supervisor of the Kemper Center for Home Gardening at the Missouri Botanical Garden. At home she gardens in a famous old wildflower garden developed by a man who made all of his own nutritious compost. "The soil here has been composted for sixty years," she says. She adds nothing to it. Meanwhile, at work at the St. Louis botanical garden, she says, "we mulch all the time with organic matter, and the percent of fertility is high."

She agrees that soluable or granular fertilizers offer a quicker source of help "if you find something looking weak or discolored and have ruled out disease and insects." A common synthetic ratio is 10-10-10, meaning 10 percent nitrogen and equal amounts of phosphorus and potassium, with the rest of the percentages as inert fill material needed to distribute the product.

Slower to work but longer lasting are some slow-release organic fertilizers, more often found in such ranges as 4-6-4 or 5-10-5. The higher phosphorus rating in the center of the three numbers is good for deep roots, says Hutson—especially important with lawn feeding if you're anticipating a summer of drought.

A word of warning: Beware of applying too much nitrogen most anytime of the year. It leads to excessive shoot and leaf growth and possibly reduced root growth. Large applications of synthetic fertilizer also may harm beneficial soil organisms.

And that brings us to other living things in soil. At the smallest, most microscopic level, certain bacteria help decompose organic matter in soil while others absorb all-important nitrogen from the air and then make the nitrogen available to plants. A type of fungus (mycorrhiza, pronounced mi-core-RI-za), meanwhile, also helps break down organic matter underground while forming symbiotic relationships with plant roots. These relationships are incredibly important to many soil scientists, who boast that the tiny threadlike fungal filaments spreading from roots out into the

Soil Solutions

Your neighborhood nursery or garden center is likely to have these solutions. If not, ask them to check out the Web site— www.hummert.com—of an international distributor of horticulture products located in St. Louis. Called, appropriately enough, Hummert International, this wholesale company celebrated its seventy-fifth anniversary in 2007. Besides carrying nearly every traditional N-P-K product imaginable, Hummert features a number of mycorrhizal products, including Transplant 1-Step, M-roots, and many more new items geared for the swelling number of home gardeners interested in organic ways of growing things. Other sources include:

- Bowood Farms (314-454-6868; www.bowoodfarms.com). This city garden center at 4605 Olive Street in St. Louis favors MycoStim, a biological soil and root innoculant containing the beneficial root-colonizing fungi of mycorrhiza. These fungi greatly increase the root's ability to take up nutrients and water, resulting in a more vigorous, stress-resistant plant.

- Soil Service Nursery (816-333-3232), 7125 Troost Avenue, Kansas City, sells Myke, a mycorrhizal product for improving soil before transplanting trees and shrubs. It is a favorite of some Kansas City master gardeners. It does not attach to roots of blueberries, rhododendrons, mountain laurels, and azaleas, says a Soil Service nurseryman.

- Worm's Way Missouri (800-285-9676; www.wormsway .com), at 1225 North Warson Road, St. Louis, sells Soil Moist with mycorrhiza.

soil greatly increase plants' abilities to absorb nutrients and water, especially in drought. Some scientists say that the mycorrhizal relationship is the most overlooked aspect of modern soil improvement. At the very least, a product with mycorrhizal fungi should be applied to soil before trees and shrubs are planted. Don't expect your own favorite 10-10-10 fertilizer to have the fungi; they're found in separate products that are not too expensive (see the "Soil Solutions" sidebar).

But healthy soils also support a teeming mass of other "beneficials." They range from tiny pest-controlling nematodes to the larger soil-aerating earthworms that deposit their castings, or rich fecal material, that provide a built-in compost. With a little time and effort, it's possible to bring almost any soil up to a botanical garden's standards.

Or as Jennifer Schutter, specialist at the Adair County Extension Center in the northern part of the state, puts it, "There are several inches of topsoil here, compared to just an inch or two" in her native Ozarks of southwest Missouri. "I would give up the good soil here for the milder climate there, so I could grow shrubs such a crape myrtle and butterfly bush, two of my favorites that typically die back in north Missouri winters. You can amend the soil," Schutter says, "but you can't amend the climate."

How to Improve Your Soil's Structure

Again, compost is key. A commercial compost du jour at a number of garden centers in Missouri is made from chunky cotton burrs, which have a significant amount of bulk for loosening clay soils, plus NPK (nitrogen, phosphorus, potassium) as well as some trace elements. Cotton once was king in the Missouri Delta. Now crops of well-composted cotton burrs come to the state from such sources as the high plains of Texas, where early freezes all but eliminate the need for the chemicals that defoliate before a cotton harvest. And cotton burr "has the advantage of particles that decompose slowly and provide some longer term benefit to soil structure than many other composts," says University of Missouri associate professor Christopher Starbuck.

Such organic matter improves heavy clay soils by binding soil particles together into "crumbs, making the soil easier to work," he says. Binding soil particles also helps improve aeration, Starbuck adds.

Worm castings and turkey manure are finding their way into compost news in Missouri. Lincoln University scientist Hwei-Yiing Johnson is studying the advantages of these different compost types, measured against her own—made from a ton or so (each week) of cafeteria food waste. She's comparing the well-rotted "cafeteria compost" to composted turkey manure as well as to commercial compost made from worm castings.

So far, says Johnson, "we recommend using turkey manure compost sparingly as a topdressing. It has the highest fertility value and pH of 8 or higher." Commercially made compost from red worm castings has a more neutral pH, "is chemically stable, and you can use a lot of it, but it's more expensive," she adds. Your own homemade compost is the cheapest source. You can make it from roughly one part grass clippings (nitrogen-rich greens) or any vegetable and fruit wastes to two parts dead leaves or sawdust and wood chips (carbon-rich browns). You can do it; it just requires situating the bin, stirring and watering it occasionally, and getting the ratio of green to brown correct for decomposition that yields the richest ingredient—"black gold," in the words of many gardeners—that you can add to your soil.

Commercial Compost Connections

Count on your favorite nursery or garden center to steer you to a good compost source. Or look in the Yellow Pages under compost and call the listed companies about the types of compost they sell as well about their products' certification by the U.S. Composting Council. Here is a sampling of five of many from around the state:

• Michael Illy Topsoil Farm, offering topsoil mixed with compost; straight compost of leaves and grass; and triple-ground mulch with compost added. 1 Illy Drive, St. Peters 63376; (636) 278-2035.

- Missouri Organic, featuring well-composted lawn, garden, and tree trimmings. 7700 East 40 Highway, Kansas City 64129; (816) 483-0908; www.missouriorganic.com.
- Morgan County Seeds, a Mennonite-operated center for garden and farm supplies plus composted turkey manure. 18761 Kelsay Road, near the geographical center of the state at Barnett 65011; (573) 378-2655; www.morgancountyseeds.com.
- St. Louis Composting, selling composted cow manure, aged yard waste, and a blend of these two, plus an all-leaf mulch compost. Three locations, including 39 Old Elam Avenue, Valley Park 63088; (636) 861-3344; www.stlcompost.com.
- Worm's Way Missouri, for many organic amendments, including ones with earthworm castings. 1225 North Warson Road, St. Louis 63132; (800) 285-9676; www.wormsway.com.

Growing Seasons

Seasonal extremes are the norm for Missouri and its gardeners. Take a recent winter, for example. Major ice storms badly "pruned" hundreds of thousands of trees, from ones in the Ozarks in southwestern Missouri to those providing canopy in and around St. Louis far to the east. Some 500,000 St. Louisans were without electricity from tree damage to electrical lines, as they had been months before when summer storms made a similar mess. And following all of that, an unusually warm March, with 80-degree highs in many areas, met up with five nights in the teens and 20s in early April. That year tornadoes and the other events meant that the St. Louis area "experienced more severe weather than any other office in the National Weather Service," says the NWS Web site.

Welcome to gardening in the Show-Me State. As state climatologist Pat Guinan puts it, Missouri's weather overall "is basically a continental climate. It's landlocked. There are no large bodies of water surrounding it." Water is slower to warm up than air and slower to cool down, he says, and so it resists temperature changes. In other words, water "tempers conditions along the coasts." For inland Missouri, with nothing to temper its climate, "there are a lot of opportunities for significant temperature changes as you go from season to season." But, he adds, those recent spring temperature shifts were unprecedented. A two-

week period from March 21 to April 3, he says, "was the third
warmest in the past 118 years. . . . The six-day period from April
4 through April 9 was the coldest ever in the past 118 years."

I'm only human. I got caught up in the early part of that
weather shift. On a warm and breezy late-March day, I put on flip
flops, a summer shirt, and jeans and drove across St. Louis to one of
my favorite garden centers to pick up a trunkload of annuals, plus a
few tropical plants. Then I got the e-mail: "If you were seduced by
the recent warm weather," said a "Frost Alert!" for subscribers to
Kansas City's www.savvygardener.com, "and planted tender items—
tomatoes, peppers, etc.—protective measures are a good idea.
Covering them with inverted flowerpots or other containers will do
the trick. For large beds, simple stakes covered with plastic or fabric
sheets in a tentlike manner will protect plantings without flattening
them." And for the first three weeks that April, while peach growers struggled with the loss of a year's production, I pulled my little
flats of plants inside at night and shuffled them back out to the deck
when temperatures allowed. You might say that I "hardened off" my
plants with all this early in-and-out activity. The experience also
hardened me to making early purchases the following spring. But
not to gardening. I'm as in love with the hobby as ever. If you can
garden here, goes the local saying, you can garden anywhere.

What Are Cold-Hardiness Zones?

These "zones" are supposed to be predictors of the tolerance of individual flowering perennials, shrubs, and trees to average lowest temperatures recorded over a specific period of time. Until recently the U.S. Department of Agriculture had the lock on creating zones that indicate how much winter cold each plant will take.

The first USDA Cold Hardiness Zone map in the 1960s became the gold standard for growers and gardeners alike. That map got revised for the USDA in 1990 by the American Horticulture Society and was revised again, by the AHS, in 2003. But the USDA raised questions about the 2003 results, took the project back—even though you still find a 2003 "Web version" of the map (under the name USDA Plant Hardiness Zone map) posted at www.usna.usda.gov/Hardzone—and started working on a new zone map. As of press time that map was unfinished. "Please remember there is no 2003 map," advises the USDA's Kim Kaplan. "That was a draft that AHS submitted that was not accepted by USDA." No map past 1990, she says, is a USDA product.

Confused? So were folks who lobbed question after question to the national Arbor Day Foundation. They wanted to know which trees would tolerate what seemed to be increasingly warmer winters. Trees, after all, are expensive items, more so than annuals or perennials. And reliable information wasn't out there, says Arbor Day spokesman Woody Nelson, especially in the face of climate change. Not waiting for an overdue update of the USDA map, he says, the Arbor Day group championed its own new map in 2006. It, too, "zones" each state by coldest temperatures—see the map at www.arborday.org/media/zones.cfm.

The Arbor Day map indicates that zones have shifted north, drawing milder climatic zones for Missouri. It puts three-quarters of the state—its entire midsection and above—in Zone 6, for plants withstanding coldest temperatures of 0 to –10 degrees. By way of comparison, the 1990 USDA map has two-thirds of

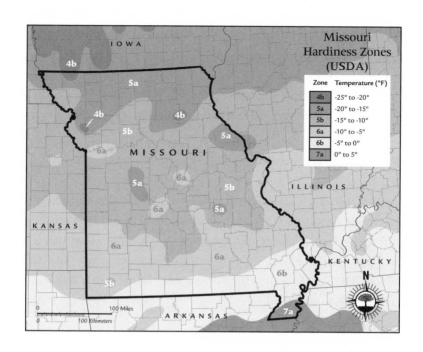

Missouri
Hardiness Zones
(USDA)

Zone	Temperature (°F)
4b	-25° to -20°
5a	-20° to -15°
5b	-15° to -10°
6a	-10° to -5°
6b	-5° to 0°
7a	0° to 5°

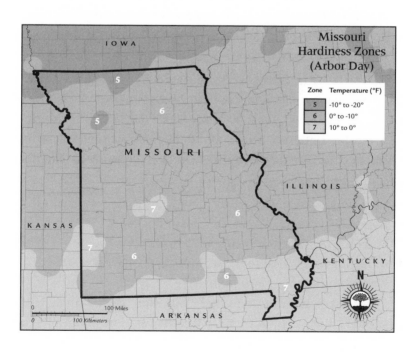

Missouri
Hardiness Zones
(Arbor Day)

Zone	Temperature (°F)
5	-10° to -20°
6	0° to -10°
7	10° to 0°

Missouri—central and most northern parts of the state—in Zone 5 (–10 to –20), with a touch of Zone 4 (–20 to –30) on the northwest border of the state, Zone 6 (0 to –10) across the bottom third, and a bit of Zone 7 (0 to 5) creeping into the Bootheel's southeast tip. See changes at www.arborday.org/media/map_change.cfm.

Which Zones Are You In?

That depends on which map you choose to look at and, then, how you decide to interpret it. If you look at the 1990 USDA hardiness zone map (which divides its zones into 5-degree subzones, "a"s and "b"s, and is based on thirteen years of weather data from 1974 to 1986), Missouri cities—generally from north to south—may get this cold in winter:

- Kirksville: Zone 5a (–15 to –20)
- Columbia: Zone 5b (–10 to –15)
- Kansas City: Zones 5b (–10 to –15) and 6a (–5 to –10)
- St. Louis: Zones 5b (–10 to –15) and 6a (–5 to –10)
- Branson: Zone 6b (0 to –5)
- Poplar Bluff: Zone 6b (0 to –5)

If you look at fifteen years of data from the national Arbor Day Foundation map, your cold-hardiness zones (divided into 10-degree increments) show a warming Kirksville, in the north-central part of the state—as much as 10 degrees warmer in winter. Missouri cities, according to the Arbor Day group, look like this:

- Kirksville: Zone 6 (0 to –10)
- Columbia: Zone 6 (0 to –10)
- Kansas City: Zone 6 (0 to –10), with pockets of 5*
- St. Louis: Zone 6 (0 to –10), with pockets of 7*
- Branson: Zone 7 (10 to 0), with pockets of 6*
- Poplar Bluff: Zone 7 (10 to 0)

An asterisk indicates that there was more than a single NCDC (National Climatic Data Center) weather station reporting, each with a different average annual low temperature, and thus more than a single zone is listed. Microclimates from urbanization or steep elevation changes make for such differences.

Are these zone designations important to you? Yes, if only because nearly every plant tag at your local nursery or garden center has a cold-hardiness zone designation printed on it. But many experts say to use the designations only as approximate starting points. Be conservative, if you really want your garden to thrive.

Zone "6 is okay, but buy for 5," is how Missouri Botanical Garden senior horticulturist Chip Tynan puts it, "the idea being to buy plants hardy to at least the next colder zone. But if you can go two zones colder, so much the better."

Agreeing wholeheartedly is Diane Peterson, a master gardener, garden-club member, and avid home gardener in the southeast Missouri town of Charleston—an easy Zone 7 on the Arbor Day map, a 6 on USDA's. And yet Peterson gardens for Zone 5. "I try not to do much outside of Zone 5—that is, if I'm counting on something staying around," she says on the day of her town's annual Dogwood-Azalea Festival, held on the third weekend of April.

Most of all, says MaryAnn Fink, coordinator of the Missouri Landscape & Nursery Association, "when you purchase a plant, understand the value of the pleasure that it gives you. And understand there's always the chance of loss. But there's also a huge chance for success, especially if you grow what's appropriate for your area. That's why we have display and trial gardens," she says of ones at Missouri's botanical gardens as well as on campuses of state and local universities (see chapter 11).

When to Choose One Map over the Other

Choose the Arbor Day map if you're planting trees, says arborist Mike Sestric, of the Kirkwood company Trees, Forests & Landscapes. The Arbor Day map was developed by a tree group in response to questions about climate change from its tree-oriented clientele. "We definitely take it into consideration," Sestric says of the foundation's map. "The climate's obviously getting warmer." The map moves most of Missouri into Zone 6, and that's the range he's seen lately in many of the state's gardens. But if homeowners are wary of that, buy for Zone 5 and experiment here and there—in a yard's warmer pockets or protected places—with plants tagged for Zone 6. Also, Sestric suggests looking at new cultivars, some from the north specially developed to take a little more heat (river birch varieties, for instance) and some magnolia species from the south that winter better farther north. The Arbor Day map "is a rule of thumb and it gives us a range, but we don't use it as our number-one guide. Each site needs to be analyzed," Sestric says. "The big news out there is microclimates."

Microclimates—Zones within Zones

Microclimates occur in many places in Missouri. A microclimate is a small area of climate that may be quite different from the larger climate around it. What causes these zones within zones? Factors include the following.

Elevation differences play a part. They may be subtle—from the highest point of Taum Sauk Mountain at 1,772 feet to the lowest point at the St. Francis River of 230 feet above sea level. But gentle hills are relentless in many areas, making for situations where cooler air from slightly higher elevations sinks into pockets below. Ten-degree differences in early morning temperatures—from the top of a hill to the bottom—aren't unusual, according to Guinan.

Urbanization is another source of these zones within zones. My own tiny city garden has a brick garage only 30 feet or so from a south-facing, two-story brick house, and tall privacy fencing all the way around. Needless to say, the brick absorbs the warmth and radiates it back, making my yard warmer than those of open, lushly planted suburban 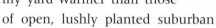 St. Louis. Beyond that, other nearby buildings, pavement, and hard, manmade surfaces also hold and reflect heat—giving some cities the unpleasant summer title of "heat islands." Take advantage of this by planting tender or experimental plants—out of your zone—in a protected area near a south-facing wall.

In Columbia, where climatologist Guinan works, the differences between urban and rural are clear. He often compares readings from a weather station on the campus of the University of Missouri there with ones from a weather station in the countryside a few miles from the city. "The annual average minimum temperatures are about a degree and a half warmer on the campus. When you look at this sort of information, it actually translates to a longer growing season in the city of about two weeks."

Sun versus shade. It's common sense that sunny spots in the garden tend to be warmer year-round. Shady ones are cooler and, in winter, cold enough that they may even keep plants dormant longer in case of an unusually late-spring frost. The PlantFinder service of the Missouri Botanical Garden—at www.mobot.org/gardeninghelp/plantfinder—gives sun, part-sun, shade, and part-shade conditions for each of its thousands of Missouri plants. If in doubt about a tender plant, says Carol Stewart, a prize-winning amateur gardener in Clayton, plant two or three of these perennials in various conditions around the garden, as she does, "to see how each does and where it does best."

Wind. Even within a single neighborhood or property, microclimates may pop up due to air flow and wind. "My own garden in Kirkwood," says horticulturist June Hutson, supervisor of the Kemper Center for Home Gardening at the Missouri Botanical Garden, "is a cold garden, with exposure to a lot of wind and low areas that frost early. I'd have to say it's Zone 5 as a sure shot."

In the face of changing national advice, Hutson suggests that homeowners "get to know your own garden, where it's warm and where it's colder. And, if you're going to shop, maybe you ought to go someplace where they know if a plant's hardy or not." The local independent garden center is a best bet, she says, especially when there are trained horticulturists on staff.

Frost Dates and Your Growing Season

What's the difference between frost, light freeze, moderate freeze, and hard freeze? You hear these terms on weather channels and in the local news. According to state climatologist Guinan, frost is a temperature low of 32 degrees. It may do minimal damage to foliage and flowers, unless it continues for several days. Foliage of perennials tends to survive this level of cold.

Light freeze is a little more worrisome. It's defined by Guinan as temperatures between 29 and 32 degrees. Tender plants may die, but there is little harm to other vegetation unless the temperature pattern continues for days. A moderate freeze happens between 25 and 28 degrees, he says. With these temperatures comes a destructive effect to some vegetation and damage to fruit blossoms and to tender plants. And a hard freeze—24 degrees or colder—is also called a "killing freeze" because temperatures drop low enough to kill much leafy growth.

Average first and last frost dates vary across the Missouri landscape. Here are a few of those average—accent on the "average"—dates: St. Joseph on Missouri's northwest border has April 20 as an average last frost date, October 10 for the average first; St. Louis gardeners, across the state to the southeast, work on the premise of an average last spring frost somewhere between April 10 to 15 and a first fall frost around October 15; Charleston, much farther to the southeast, at the top of the Bootheel, has a last average frost date of April 5 and first frost date somewhere around October 30.

Freeze and Thaw

Wide temperature swings—as are common in Missouri—may cause damage to perennials that otherwise are hardy for the region. This can happen when water in the soil freezes and thaws—expanding and contracting. Such actions sometimes push roots and crowns upwards in a process called heaving. And when that happens, exposed plant parts may get damaged or die from cold temperatures and drying winds. Most prone to heaving are plants with shallow root systems or ones planted so late in the season that their root systems haven't fully established. Mulching after the first hard frost—with at least 3 inches of compost, chopped leaves, or pine needles, for instance—helps keep ground temperatures from swinging as wildly as air temperatures do. But keep an eye on plants throughout the winter, and reapply mulch as needed.

Measuring Missouri's Summer Heat and Humidity

Summers can feel like a blast furnace in Missouri. The warmest on record were in the 1930s, says Guinan, with more than forty days of 100-degree heat during the summer of 1936. "Being a climatologist and looking at trends over the past 112 years," Guinan says, "I've always been firm believer if it happened before, it can happen again. We have not had an exceptionally hot summer in the last twenty-five years." Humidity during the summertime also can get oppressive in the state. "We're pretty much similar to locations on the Gulf Coast, when the Bermuda high builds in across the southeast U.S. and circulation on that high is clockwise and pumps up that Gulf of Mexico moisture into Missouri."

Enter yet another map, this one for heat zones. Do you need to use it? This is a mapping exercise by the American Horticulture Society and one that is used less frequently than the winter-oriented USDA Cold Hardiness Zone map. Heat doesn't kill as frequently as does extreme cold, or drought, for that matter. But heat is a factor, says Alan Branhagen, horticulture director of Powell Gardens at Kingsville, near Kansas City. "What I like about the AHS Heat-Zone map is that it shows we—Kansas City and St. Louis—are in the same summer heat zone with southern cities including Nashville, Atlanta, Charlotte, and Washington, D.C.," says Branhagen. "That summer heat allows for extensive growth in tropical plants and hardens off some otherwise marginally hardy plants like southern and sweet bay magnolias."

The heat map is based on the average number of days above 86 degrees—temperatures at which plants suffer damage to cells— each year. Most of the state is listed in Heat Zone 7, with 60 to 90 days over this critical temperature. Southeastern Missouri is in Heat Zone 8 (90 to 120 days), and a dozen of the northern counties are rated cooler, in Heat Zone 6 (45 to 60 days above 86 degrees). You can view this map at www.ahs.org/pdfs/05_heat _map.pdf.

Plants for Hot Places

What plants best take the state's summer heat and humidity? When temperatures soar above 86 degrees for many days in a row, plants often take a hit. They may not show damage right away as with a freeze, but they're likely to begin a slow decline until temperatures cool again. Keep them well watered. And consider moving sun-loving containers into partial shade until hot weather breaks. Also, using plants that take Missouri's heat is an important tactic.

Ferns do well here, especially the native ones. They're made for shade and for damper conditions. Other natives, too, are built for full-on sun as well as for shade and the soils, the heat, and the dense, moist air (see more about native plants in chapter 6). The cultivated varieties of hosta for shade, plus daylilies for sun, and even ground covers of the genus *Ajuga* valiantly resist muggy, hot weather. Certain herbs—basil especially—love hot weather. And when watered and otherwise properly cared for, most annuals— think lantana, sunflower, morning glory vine—and nearly all tropicals thrive in Missouri's summers.

A great overall program on what to grow in such conditions is called Athens Select, named after the city of Athens, Georgia, in which its founder, horticulturist Allan Armitage, tests annuals for heat and humidity tolerance. Armitage's trial gardens are located on the grounds of the University of Georgia. He frequently visits Missouri gardens and nurseries, and his beautiful new plant varieties each year are huge hits with master gardeners and amateur gardeners alike. Meanwhile, a portion of the proceeds from the sale of each Athens Select plant goes to the university to help fund continued plant research. For a full list of new introductions, plus the nurseries and greenhouses in Missouri that carry these plants, go to www.athensselect.com.

Extending Your Growing Seasons

From small water-filled containers to cold frames, hoop houses, and even small greenhouses, there are ways to trick plants into thinking they're in slightly warmer climes. Among water-filled containers is a brand that's famous among tomato growers called Wall-O-Water. It is a season-extending circle of plastic tubes that, when filled with water and put around a tender tomato transplant, gives that plant the protection of sun-warmed water through cool spring nights and as much as a three-week jump on tomatoes that otherwise don't go in the ground until mid-May.

Cold frames are small structures that can be made from old window frames hinged to wooden boxes. They sit on the ground and protect transplants and potted plants when sun hits the glass and warms what's underneath on a cool spring day. The frame then holds heat through the night. Hinges let a gardener lift the glass if temperatures get too high during the day. Hoop houses work on the same principle: A series of large hoops or half circles made of plastic pipe or metal and covered tightly with a plastic sheeting gets heated by the sun and cooled by the wind. Soils, and plants, underneath the sheeting are heated and cooled, too. The plastic may be raised on either side during the day for ventilation.

Small greenhouses may seem an extravagance but are as inexpensive as a homemade, clear-plastic lean-to for propping up against the side of a house and as costly as an all-glass framed structure that's like a new room added to home or garden. Growers of orchids and other tropicals may see the need for this extreme protection. But the average home gardener is more likely to use something smaller. See the excellent guide by University of Missouri Extension called *Building and Using Hotbeds and Coldframes* at http://extension.missouri.edu/explore/agguides/hort/g06965.htm.

CHAPTER THREE

Water

Missouri is a deceptively large place. The distance between the northwest and southeast corners of the state, says Missouri state climatologist Pat Guinan, is the same as from two famously shaped regions—the southernmost tip of the Missouri Bootheel to the edge of the Florida Panhandle. And so rainfall conditions can be drastically different across this deep, wide region. They range from the generally too-dry north, central, and southwest parts of Missouri to the often overly wet Mississippi River valley of the southeast. "To throw out a blanket statement," says Guinan, "typically the northwest corner of the state gets 35 inches of rain and to the southeast, 50 inches. On average, and annually, there's about a 15-inch difference."

Watering priorities, too, are very different, depending on where in Missouri you live. Portions of the western side of the state, including St. Joseph, Kansas City, and Springfield, have suffered from varying degrees of severe, even extreme, drought in recent years. During a recent summer, Springfield's city council voted in voluntary limits to lawn irrigation and car washing if water storage at area lakes drop to 60 percent, with mandatory limits at 50 percent and below. During another period of drought in the state capital of Jefferson City, residents also were asked to conserve water. St. Louis, on the east-central border, has stayed a bit less dry, showing up on drought maps intermittently as abnormally dry or, occasionally, in moderate drought conditions. But its location on major rivers has meant there've been no water restrictions there, not even residential metering of water within the city limits.

Missouri's Rainfall Averages

Taken city by city, Missouri's annual rainfall figures look wildly different. In one recent year, for instance, one of the southeastern-most cities near the Arkansas border, Poplar Bluff, recorded a whopping 65 inches of rain and melted snow, while Kansas City—

Whether Weather

Here are a few of state climatologist Pat Guinan's top sources for up-to-date rain information:

National Weather Service Precipitation Analysis (www.srh.noaa.gov/rfcshare/precip_analysis_new.php). "I really like this site," says Guinan. "You can click on Missouri and overlay roads, towns, and a legend to estimate rainfall for the past twenty-four hours, or the past month, or the year to date. You get a nice feel for who's been receiving rain."

Community Collaborative Rain, Hail & Snow Network (www.cocorahs.org). This network of volunteer weather observers started in Colorado and has gone nationwide, says Guinan. He is co-coordinator for Missouri. "It's a nice resource," he says. "Over two hundred people are reporting daily with rain gauges in every county. It really picked up in 2006 when every office of the Farm Service Agency in Missouri came on board."

U.S. Drought Monitor Map (www.drought.unl.edu/dm/monitor.html). There's growing interest in the weekly national updates—in map and text form—of the National Drought Mitigation Center, headquartered at the University of Nebraska–Lincoln. Go to the drought-monitor map and click on Missouri for a more detailed look at drought trends across the entire Midwest. "They keep improving that product every year," says Guinan. "It uses all sorts of expertise, and the USDA has embraced it for drought information."

far to the north and west—got 31 inches of both types of precipitation. St. Louis, to the east, had close to its average, with 30 inches of rain and 11 of the white stuff. St. Louis' normal precipitation—from records averaged over a period of thirty years—is a total of 38¾ inches. As of a recent spring, meanwhile, "drought was eliminated in the entire state due to a fairly wet winter," says Guinan. "Winter is a good time in Missouri to recharge moisture levels, above- and belowground. Evaporation is minimal, vegetation is dormant, and that all provides the opportunity for moisture to get into the soil." But dry conditions, he says, are tricky to work with and, especially, to predict. "Drought can be very interesting," he says. "It can be random and highly localized." Even back in 1993, when the mother of all floods brought the Missouri and Mississippi Rivers up and far out of their banks, "believe or not," says Guinan, the southeasternmost Bootheel was in a rainfall deficit.

How Much Water Do Your Plants Need?

Different climates and soils—and, indeed, different types of plants—dictate a range of watering needs and techniques.

Climatic conditions clearly can make a big difference in Missouri gardens. And gardeners who closely monitor rain patterns are always a step ahead. Generally speaking, the majority of lawns and gardens in the state need a minimum of 1 to 1½ inches of rain—or irrigation—each week. A way to monitor that water is with an inexpensive rain gauge, purchased at a local garden center, hardware, or feed and seed store. Even easier is to plop a clean tunafish can—measuring almost exactly 1½ inches from top to bottom—out where rain or a sprinkler hits it reliably. Check the gauge or can every few days until a week passes to know whether or not to water your in-ground plants.

Container plantings have different water needs entirely. Containers typically get potted with fast-draining, soilless mixtures and then are plopped onto sun-drenched patios or porches.

They may dry out especially fast in wind. And if porous clay pots are used, even more water evaporates from the sides of the pots. The advice in summer is to water containers thoroughly once a day until water runs out the bottom but not to let water stand in any saucers the pots might sit in. And a second time daily, in the heat of a Missouri July or August, check soil an inch below the surface and water again if that soil is dry.

Soil types in the garden make a big difference when watering. If your garden soil is full of clay, overwatering is a problem because the soil already is dense—with limited space, or "pores," for much-needed air in the soil. Too much water in clay is likely to push out the oxygen, leaving plant roots to struggle, even to suffocate and die. Sandy soils, on the other hand, are susceptible to drought and may not get watered enough. Even with a good watering, they tend to dry out rapidly. An inch or so of water on a sandy soil will percolate down a foot or more; that same amount on a clay soil will reach down only 5 or 6 inches.

No Bathtubs Here

Before gardening directly in Missouri's ubiquitous clay soil, consider adding such organic matter as compost, well-aged manure, or peat moss to a wide area around each plant, says Jeff Oberhaus, owner of Vintage Hill Farms garden center in Franklin. Otherwise the hole that you dig in clay may become a "bathtub," he says, when water fills in around good soil at the roots, only to hit clay walls at the edge of the hole. Better, and easier, Oberhaus says, is to "create a raised planting area. This does not have to be a berm or require landscape timbers or retaining walls. Adding a 6- to 10-inch layer of good topsoil is ample for most plants to get a good start, and they can gradually extend roots into the native soil to help anchor them."

Know your soil. But again, a very general rule of thumb is to give your garden an inch or so of water each week and then let the soil partially dry out before the next round of watering.

Type of plants. If you're xeriscaping in the dry weather of Springfield, as several master gardeners there do, you're going to want plants that require only ½ inch of water a week (daylilies, salvia, echinacea, phlox) or, better yet, ones that require little or no watering. These xeric plants—named after the Greek word for dry, *xeros*—include cacti, Russian sage, lavender, sedum, nepeta, goldenrod, and feather reed grass. Master Gardeners of Southwest Missouri maintain a xeriscape garden in Springfield's Phelps Grove Park that teaches homeowners, in this sometimes drought-stricken part of the state, how to get blooms beyond such water-needy plants as roses, hibiscus, and lilacs. Go to www.ozarks gardens.com and click on Real Gardens to see three types of plantings with very different water needs.

How to Apply That Water

By hand. There's no getting around it. Some people find a daily dose of hand watering most therapeutic. They get lost in the needs of their beautiful plants and forget the cares of the day. The downside to hand watering plants in the ground is that it's not measurable and may be too shallow an application, done too often and leading to shallow roots. Successful hand watering of in-ground plants is done once a week or so with water applied thoroughly to each section of the garden, or even to each plant, according to its water needs—more water for lobelia, for instance, less for heuchera. Hand watering of containers is a different story. It needs to be done at least once a day in summer.

Sprinklers. Some gardeners recoil at the thought of watering their plants from above. They imagine fungi and powdery mildew just waiting to attack wet leaves. Many Missouri gardeners say that if you water early in the day, you should have plenty of time for foliage to dry so that chances of disease diminish. And if you do that kind of overhead watering early, and just once a week— with a deep soaking each time—there's bound to be dry foliage during the rest of the week. However, lack of good air circulation may be even more of a problem for plants prone to powdery mildew. Generally in such cases you want to strategically prune surrounding vegetation to allow for more sun and air. Also look into plant varieties bred to resist powdery mildew. Individual listings on the PlantFinder Web site of the Missouri Botanical Garden (www.mobot.org) report when powdery mildew is a problem.

Soaker hoses are flexible tubes that come complete with hundreds of tiny holes that allow water to seep out into the soil in perennial and annual beds. No foliage is harmed in this process. These hoses are wrapped around plants or lined up in narrow rows between plants and, generally, mulched over. They avoid sprinkler-system issues of overspray, runoff, and evaporation.

When to . . . *water*

Don't count on a dry surface of the soil to tell you that you
need to water. Take a trowel and dig deep in the garden. If
soil is dry several inches down, water slowly and deeply until a
rain gauge or tin can measures an inch. And do only that
much watering once a week, depending on weather.

However, soaker hoses are not designed to target specific plants.
They soak entire areas.

Drip irrigation is better able to get water directly to the root
systems of specific plants. Like soaker hoses, it conserves water
that would be lost to evaporation or runoff during overhead
watering. For vegetable gardens, for instance, drip tape—a flat
tape that expands when filled with water—generally has 12-inch
spacings between "dripper" devices inserted into the tape. And in

even rows of vegetable plants spaced a foot apart, each plant's root zone is directly targeted with water.

Drip emitter devices also target root zones directly and are more sophisticated versions in the drip-irrigation panoply of gardening solutions. They were developed in the daunting climates of Israel and South Africa, where tiny amounts of water per plant promote good growth. Kits for such irrigation include, at the very least, a control valve, supply line, lateral lines, and emitters that get spaced some 18 inches apart on the lines. Such drip devices need to be activated for a little more than an hour every week to get the recommended inch of water that supplements rainfall. But the systems are somewhat complicated and include even more equipment options. Check with staff at your favorite independent garden center. Or take a look at Robert Kourik's book on the topic, *Drip Irrigation for Every Landscape and All Climates* (Metamorphic Press).

The Art of Watering—One Woman's Story

Ellen Barredo, a horticulturist at Bowood Farms garden center in St. Louis, uses a low-tech method to water her Wildwood fescue lawn and perennial garden. Here's how.

"I still prefer once-a-week watering with a sprinkler," says Barredo, "really deep watering to develop a deeper root system so when it does get dry, you won't have a lawn that dries up immediately." And so, in each of four locations around the yard, she has either a fan-type or impulse sprinkler head permanently placed. In the evening she moves a single hose to one of those sprinkler heads for a half hour of watering. For each of the next three nights, she moves the hose again. Barredo combines the task with something pleasant—a half hour of outdoor grilling. While dinner smokes, part of her soil gets soaked, and Barredo relaxes with iced tea and takes in the garden.

Several years ago she made sure that the clay soil on her property got improved with cotton-burr compost and Turface—a product of tiny, kiln-dried clay pellets—"for quicker water penetration down to deep roots," she says. She sometimes puts out an inch-deep pie pan to confirm that she's watering at least an inch a week. Meanwhile, soil under her shrubs and other foundation plantings soak a few hours each week with a permanently installed soaker hose. "The hardest place to water," Barredo says, "is along a foundation. You don't want a sprinkler system there. Concrete can take up the water at an amazing rate."

Right Plant, Right Place?

One of the most exciting water-related programs in Missouri is Kansas City's 10,000 Rain Gardens initiative. The plan is to coax upwards of ten thousand homes, businesses, churches, and other groups to install small, shallow basin gardens, each with a very special purpose. That is, to plant wet or moist areas with native plants—ones that tolerate both wet and dry conditions and that have deep root systems to help channel storm-water runoff deep into the ground. Rain gardens absorb as much as 30 percent more water than comparable parcels of flat turf, say the experts. To date, more than a thousand Kansas City gardeners believe it, with at least that many involved in getting rain gardens started there. A big campaign lies ahead.

Here's how it began. Gardeners and environmentalists alike have long known that when Kansas City gets downpours, the city's aging storm-water system takes a big hit. It floods. Or it clogs. Or soil, fertilizers, and other chemicals wash into its waterways. The estimate to fix the system is upwards of $3.5 to $5.5 billion, says David Dods, a Kansas City environmental engineer. Lynn Hinkle saw in this not a negative but a positive for the city. She is a marketing professional who became project manager for the three-year-old rain-gardens program. "These are twenty-first-century victory gardens," Hinkle says, likening the hundreds of new rain

Rain-Garden Reviewing

For much more information on whether a rain garden's for you, go to:

- 10,000 Rain Gardens, a Web site devoted to this new Kansas City project at www.rainkc.com.

- Critical Site, Prairie & Wetland Center, billing itself as "the Midwest's largest producer of native plants, trees, and shrubs," at www.critsite.com.

- Grow Native!, the Missouri Conservation Department's innovative program with a Web site showing Missouri native plant species, landscape designs, and where to buy native plant products and services at www.grownative.org. And free at www.mdcnatureshop.com or by calling toll-free (877) 521-8632 is *Native Plant Rain Gardens,* telling you how to use native plants to soak up storm water and create wildlife habitat.

- *Rain Gardens: Bringing Water to Life in the Designed Landscape,* by Nigel Dunnett and Andy Clayden (Timber Press, 2007); an even newer book co-authored by Kansas City environmental engineer David Dods, along with Rusty Schmidt and Dan Shaw, is *The Blue Thumb Guide to Raingardens, Design and Installation for Homeowners in the Upper Midwest,* available online at www.terracehorticulturalbooks.com.

- Shaw Nature Reserve Web site (www.shawnature.org) for, among other helpful tips, a *Native Landscaping Manual* that lists Missouri garden designers who have a subspecialty in rain gardens and includes instructions on doing the work yourself.

gardens around the city to the World War II vegetable beds that helped feed a sacrificing nation. "We're giving people a way to connect with the issues and with the greater community," she says.

JoAnne Owens believes this to be true. She helps with the Visitation Catholic Church rain garden on Main Street just south of downtown Kansas City. She also is business manager at the church. "We opened our new building in 2004," she says, "and the city required this detention pond for overflow from the storm sewer system. It was unsightly, mucky, and usually full of water." Conservation ecologist Laurie Brown, with Patti Banks Associates, helped the church design a rain garden in that space, with native plants purchased from a major purveyor called Critical Site, Prairie & Wetland Center, in Belton, a southern suburb of Kansas City.

The church's shallow basin-shaped space was cleared and no conditioning of the soil required. Native-soil-loving plants went in. They have deep roots that help water filter down through the soil. In this garden they include the rose pink summer flowers of marsh milkweed (*Asclepias incarnata*), orange coneflower (*Rudbeckia fulgida*), bright purple blue blooms of mist flower (*Eupatorium coelestinum*), showy yellow lanceleaf coreopsis (*Coreopsis lanceolata*), moisture-loving blue flag iris (*Iris virginica* var. *shrevei*) and fall-blooming blue lobelia (*Lobelia siphilitica*). "After a rain, it drains within twenty-four hours," eliminating the fears of mosquitoes, she adds. "Neighborhood, parishioners, and I are extremely happy. We have been on garden tours, the water department has had rain-garden training sessions here. We couldn't be happier."

Mulch Madness

After amending soil, planting your plants, and installing irrigation, mulch is next. And it's supremely important, at a moderate rate of 2 to 3 inches deep. In spring it decreases evaporation of water, it discourages competition from unsightly weeds, and it brings a sense of unity to the landscape. In late fall, after a first frost, it keeps soil temperatures evenly cold and protects roots from heaving after a period of freeze and thaw.

Best mulches made in Missouri include compost, ground-up hardwood, wood chips, pine bark such as you find in better potting soils, even pine needles, the latter especially good for acid-loving plants. Or go to http://extension.missouri.edu and type "mulch" into the search field.

Retail sources of mulch include nearly every garden center in the state. Here are just three:

- **Missouri Organic,** 7700 East 40 Highway, Kansas City; (816) 483-0908; www.missouriorganic.com. Offering hardwood chips and a variety of other mulches, plus an online materials calculator to show how much mulch is needed for certain areas.

- **Moffet Nursery & Garden Shop,** 6451 State Route 6 NE, St. Joseph; (816) 233-1223. They feature a triple-ground, mostly oak mulch called Ozark Black. It's sold in bulk, not in more convenient bag form, and yet "it's rapidly becoming our best seller," says Moffet president and landscape architect Bob Stubblefield. It breaks down like compost, he adds, and is good for the garden, "especially if your soil is terrible." But don't pile it, or any mulch, on thick. Two inches is fine, he says. "I'd rather they'd do no mulch than too much. That's a pet peeve of mine. Roots, not only of trees but of any plant, breathe just as you and I do. And mulch too close to the base of trees can loosen the bark and allow insects to get underneath."

- **Total Environments Garden Center,** 804 Old Highway 63 North, Columbia; (573) 874-8690. They carry a new mulch that's growing in popularity—pine straw or pine needle mulch from the central and southern parts of the state. It works well around acid-loving plants. In 2007, the second year for sales, twice as much went home with retail customers as did in 2006.

Green Things

Annuals and Tropicals

Perennials may have come of age in Missouri in the 1980s and '90s, when growers packed garden centers with thousands of never-before-seen hybrids. But now many home-based gardens are maturing, while gardeners look to fill in blank spots or to add color to decks, patios, condos, and window boxes with long-flowering annuals. And these aren't simply the geraniums, begonias, or petunias that Aunt Evie used to plant around the lamppost. New annuals and tropicals are like their perennial cousins—high-tech cultivars or recent discoveries from here and around the world—all designed to make lush new gardening statements. Think bacopa, laurentia, scaevola, diascia, and cuphea. You'll find a few, or all, of these in garden centers across the state.

What Exactly Is an Annual?

An annual, in very simple terms, is one of nature's comeback kids. It's a plant that has a one-year life cycle, from seed in spring to blooms in summer to seeds set from those blooms before the plant dies with frost in fall. A soft-stemmed, herbaceous perennial may "die" back to the ground in winter, but it returns in spring from roots, tubers, and rhizomes living underground. An annual, on the other hand, must return reliably from seed. And that's why they flower so profusely; they must do so to produce that all-important, self-perpetuating seed.

Most annuals fall into several subcategories. To make things simple, let's call the basic categories cool-weather annuals and warm-weather annuals.

Cool-weather annuals also get termed hardy and half-hardy annuals because they can tolerate very cool temperatures. For the hardiest of all in Missouri, think of the pansy (*Viola* x *wittrockiana*) and Johnny-jump-up (*V. tricolor*). They may be planted outside in fall—in a protected place, with good mulching and good luck—to flower even more beautifully the following spring. Or there are the cool-weather annuals, such as flowering cabbage (*Brassica oleracea*), that do better when it's cooler than when the heat cranks up. Even the twining, cascading nasturtium (*Tropaeolum majus*) and sweet pea (*Lathyrus odoratus*) easily take off from seed as early as April in Missouri and tolerate cool weather, only to fade as heat and humidity do them in. Keys to helping hardy, cold-tolerant annuals beat the heat are to provide some afternoon shade and to keep their well-drained soils evenly moist and mulched.

Warm-weather annuals for Missouri tend to be natives of such sunny climes as Madagascar, Southeast Asia, Africa, and the subtropical Americas. Think of the hummingbird favorite that is red-blossomed cypress vine, also called cardinal climber (*Ipomoea quamoclit*). It loves sun and heat, as do other annuals in this category. However, as an example of how every plant is just a little bit different, wishbone flower (*Torenia fournieri*) is one warm-weather annual that may need part shade in the hottest summers that Missouri has to offer.

Tender perennials are a quite common subcategory of annuals. Sweet potato vine (*Ipomoea batatas*), for instance, is ubiquitous now in Missouri containers and garden beds and is thought of as an annual. However, it is winter hardy in warmer parts of the country. In Missouri it may be overwintered in the sense that its tubers may be dug from the soil before the last frost, dried, and stored in a little dry peat or vermiculite in a cool part of the house. Coleus and lantana also are tender perennials that may be brought back to life the next gardening season. The latter may be overwintered indoors after it's cut back by one-third in the fall and sprayed with insecticidal soap; the former, coleus, may best be overwintered by taking cuttings in summer and rooting them directly in water or moist potting soil.

Biennials have "bi" in their name because they live for two years, growing from seed to a vegetative state the first year, blooming and setting seed the second year before they die. Typically home gardeners find these as plants in nurseries after the first year of growth and treat them as annuals. Examples of biennials are foxglove, sweet william, narrow-leaved mullein (*Verbascum* hybrids), and, less frequently found, hesperis or dame's rocket (*Hesperis matronalis*).

Tropicals are just that—plants native to the hottest spots on earth. They were fashionable during Victorian times. Cannas, palms, and elephant ears, especially, graced the grounds of the Missouri Botanical Garden in St. Louis throughout the era of Victoriana. And as part of that botanical garden's celebration of its 150th anniversary in 2009, tropicals are plantings that will help re-create the garden's early grandeur. Tropicals are growing in popularity in Missouri home gardens not only for their wild flowers and exotic foliage but also because they take the state's relentless summer heat and humidity better than almost any other "annual" plant. They're also relatively easy to winter indoors, as bulbs and tubers stored in a cool dry place, or as plants kept on sunny windowsills.

Annuals to Start Easily from Seed

Zinnias, zinnias, and more zinnias, say many gardeners in Missouri. Zinnias arguably are the easiest flowers to grow from seed—either indoors before the last frost or right in the ground in late spring. And the best part about starting these annuals from their little featherweight, arrowhead-shaped seeds is that they come in a much wider variety from seed companies than from transplants. So popular is zinnia, by the way, that the National Garden Bureau named it the plant of the year in 2000. Independent plant testers, called All-America Selections (www.aaswinners.com), picked two zinnias back-to-back for national "flower winners" in 2005 ('Magellan Coral') and 2006 ('Zowie! Yellow Flame'). Still other plants to try from seed include the pink-, rose-, and white-blooming cosmos; all manner of golden yellow sunflowers; 'Heavenly Blue' morning glory vines; and twining orange and yellow nasturtiums. See the National Garden Bureau fact sheets at www.ngb.org for some seed-starting advice.

For sources of great seed for annuals, you can go to local, independent garden centers or online to such national and international sources as Park Seed Co. (www.parkseed.com), Thompson & Morgan (www.thompson-morgan.com), Johnny's Selected Seeds (www.johnnyseeds.com), and Renee's Garden Seeds (www.reneesgarden.com). But consider a fast-growing, relatively new Missouri source of annuals seed stock—Baker Creek

Heirloom Seeds (www.rareseeds.com), located 45 miles east of Springfield. At the very least, go online to view some of the Baker Creek annuals or to order a free seed catalog.

Jere Gettle is the remarkable young man who started the Baker Creek business when he was just seventeen. His family had moved from Montana to Missouri's Ozark region, where the weather's warmer, he says, and farmland more reasonably priced. Gettle collected the seeds of yellow tomatoes, pink banana squash, and other unusual plants that his parents and grandparents grew. He became so interested that at age sixteen he joined the not-for-profit, heirloom-oriented Seed Savers Exchange

(www.seedsavers.org). A year later he printed 550 copies of his first, twelve-page seed catalog. By 2007, his tenth anniversary in the business, his colorful eighty-four-page Baker Creek Heirloom Seed catalog contained some one thousand varieties of annual flowers and vegetables from seeds collected around the world and grown, for Gettle, on a network of farms. The catalog went out to ninety thousand interested gardeners, says Gettle, who also hosts an annual spring heirloom seed festival on his farm in Mansfield, complete with old-time music and sales of seeds, plants, and food. His festivals draw some five thousand folks from Missouri, Arkansas, and a number of other states.

Annuals to Buy as Transplants

Impatiens, begonias, coleus, geraniums, and ornamental sweet potato vines are not so easily started from seed. Propagation from

Top Heirloom Flowers to Start from Seed

Jere Gettle, heirloom-seed phenom from Missouri's Baker Creek Heirloom Seeds company, shares his top picks of seed-grown heirloom flowers:

Amaranthus, or love-lies-bleeding (*Amaranthus caudatus*), produces red ropelike flowers and is one of Gettle's favorite crops. It yields plenty of seeds, he says, and is a very old heirloom, dating to before 1700.

Hollyhock 'Jet Black' (*Alcea rosea*) is from a variety planted at Monticello by Thomas Jefferson, according to Gettle. But it is a new, dark color for Baker Creek. "Our main growth," Gettle says of his business, "is our deep-colored vegetables and flowers."

Kiss-me-over-the-garden-gate (*Polygonum orientale*) has long, arching pink flower heads. Some of these plants reach 6 feet tall. "Freeze seeds first for a few weeks before planting," says Gettle. "If you don't, you're not going to get good germination."

Mexican sunflower (*Tithonia rotundifolia*) produces masses of orange red blooms for most of the summer season. "They do incredibly well for us."

Morning glory 'Clark's Heavenly Blue' (*Ipomoea* hybrid) dates to the 1920s, says Gettle, and features 4-inch-wide blue flowers on 12-foot vines.

Zinnia 'Envy' (*Zinnea elegans*) may be newer than some of Gettle's aged heirlooms, but its chartreuse blooms "are really different, bright, and cheerful," he says, "and in our climate it seems to be very resistant to powdery mildew."

stem cuttings of these plants is preferred. Buying them outright as transplants in spring is easiest. And petunias, says Missouri seed expert Jere Gettle of Mansfield, "are tricky ones, with very tiny seeds. Petunias are not hard to grow from seeds," he adds, "but the seeds are just like a fine dust that most gardeners won't want to deal with."

When shopping for annual transplants, look for healthy, green foliage and generous root systems. Don't be afraid to lift plants very gently from their trays, six-packs, or plastic pots to inspect the roots. A good garden center's staff will understand. Consider walking past plants already in flower to go for ones that are sturdy looking but haven't yet bloomed. The soon-to-bloom are concentrating more energy on developing sound root systems and are saving themselves for the flowers they'll produce once established in your garden.

Best Annuals for Missouri

The following lists barely scratch the surface of excellent plants that thrive in Missouri soils, or in containers, throughout summer months. And the sources mentioned here are just a few of many that you may know or find online. These annuals are divided into two lists—ones that are tried and true but that also have been improved in recent years, and ones that you may not know of or only have just begun to grow.

The Classics, with a Twist

Asclepias curassavica is a plant of many names—scarlet milkweed, silkweed, and Mexican blood flower among them. It's a major nectar source for monarch butterflies, and it blooms for a much longer period than does its cousin, the perennial milkweed in Missouri. Ornamental gardeners are interested in two stellar new cultivars of this tender perennial—'Silky Gold', with brilliant orange yellow color, and 'Silky Red', with deep red flower clusters. The plant self-seeds, but not in an invasive way. It recently made the list of fifty or so top plants for Missouri in the annually updated Plants of Merit listing—see www.plantsofmerit.org.

Begonia, that trusted, old, waxy-foliage plant that tolerates sun or shade (*Begonia* x *semperflorens-cultorum*), is a standard in many traditional gardens. You've seen its rounded little mounds repeated alongside walkways, looking like little dark green, red-capped soldiers in a row. But when 'Dragon Wing' begonias (*B.* x *argenteoguttata*) hit the garden centers in recent years, the average home gardener sensed that something was up. Did hybridizers get their hands on an old friend? Not exactly. The 'Dragon Wing' is a distant cousin. But so popular is the new, shade-loving tender perennial 'Dragon Wing Red'—with scarlet blossoms and leaves that look like they're ready to take flight—that it's been graduated to "emeritus" status on the Missouri Botanical Garden's Plants of

Merit list. Check out the American Begonia Society (www.begonias .org) for more.

Canna is so old it's new again. Pick any one of the many varieties of this tropical plant, grown from bulblike rhizomes, and you have a stunning centerpiece to a container or to a hot-colored garden bed. *Canna* 'Pretoria' is a favorite, with green-and-yellow striped leaves and flashy orange blossoms. But check out the new, dwarf *C.* 'Lucifer', with robust growth, dark green foliage, and striking red flowers edged in gold. Both cannas are among Powell Gardens' recommended cultivars, also including 'Cleopatra', 'Tropicana', and 'Rosamond Cole'. See more at www.powell gardens.org.

Coleus was king when Queen Victoria reigned. This mostly foliage plant had been brought to England by traders from Africa and Indonesia, and it made a showy presence alongside palms and cannas in conservatories of the day. But it lost its lustrous color in sun. Over the years hybridizers fussed with new leaf textures and hues. In recent years an amazing sun tolerance has been built into new "sun coleus" varieties. But the breeders can't stop experimenting. The new Kong series brings coleus back to king-size status, with extralarge leaves and stature. It's also partial to shade. Kong, says Ann Lapedis of Sugar Creek Gardens in Kirkwood (www.sugarcreekgardens.com), is a boon for folks who need tropicals that are large and colorful enough to have a big impact in shady garden beds.

Geranium, the common, mop-headed annual, is not a *Geranium* at all but a *Pelargonium.* True geraniums are cold hardy and shade loving. Plants of the *Pelargonium* genus, on the other hand, are annuals commonly called geraniums that love a daily dose of sun. You see them by the thousands in pots along European windowsills. Red still is the top-requested color. But new hues— think violet or salmon—come out every year. And so-called "zonal geraniums"—with zonelike gold and silver lines around their leaves but less-showy flowers—are increasingly popular for eye-catching

containers. See the Web site of the International Geranium Society (www.intgeraniumsoc.com) for more.

Impatiens have it made in the shade. They are nearly everywhere in yards where sun doesn't shine and yet summer color is called for. Super Elfin and Sultana are names of the popular annual bedding plants (*Impatiens walleriana*). But the real news in impatiens are the sun-tolerant varieties—principally the 'Sunny Lady' hybrids. Take a look at them on the Parks Seed Web site (www.parkseed.com) for such descriptions as "the most heat-tolerant impatiens ever grown." Or go to the site of Cottage Garden (www.cottgardens.com), just across the Mississippi River from St. Louis, for an extended list of new varieties.

Lantana does exceptionally well in Missouri's summer heat, planted in the ground or in containers. And butterflies love to feed from its colorful, flat-blossomed landing pads. New varieties that perform at the top of their class in Missouri Botanical Garden 2006 Flowering Annuals Performance Trials (see www.mobot.org/gardeninghelp/plantinfo.shtml) are *Lantana camara* 'Pinata', in pale pinks and yellows, plus the aptly named 'Peach Surprise' and 'Landmark Rose Glow'. And a new series called Tiddley Winks is a lantana to keep an eye on.

Pansies (*Viola* x *wittrockiana*) are where Missouri gardeners make a big mistake each year, says Chris Schaul, owner of Wine

Country Gardens in Defiance (http://winecountrygardens.net). "Make room for pansies in the fall, not in spring," she says. These cool-weather annuals thrive in fall's air temperatures and summer-warmed soils. They get established—with the help of a little Osmocote—and if mulched properly will overwinter just fine. "And then the spring is so much prettier," she says, with pansies returning even bigger and better than in fall. More pansy information may be found in the Missouri Botanical Garden's online Pansy Cultivar Ratings at www.mobot.org/plantinfo.shtml.

Petunia hybrids are so ubiquitous and well publicized that you couldn't imagine anything new. The trademarked Wave series, for instance, stole the spotlight in garden centers when the low-mounding, spreading, heat-tolerant 'Wave Blue' was first introduced. It won a flower of the year award in 2003 from the independent All-America Selections. And new Wave colors or Wave types keep on coming. But Supertunias, says Ann Lapedis of Sugar Creek Gardens in Kirkwood, "are better than Waves, with masses of flowers, and they just don't stop until they're completely covered." The new 'Supertunia Vista Bubblegum' is a favorite of many of her customers.

Portulaca grandiflora moss rose, with satiny little rose-colored flowers on low-growing, fleshy stems and succulent-like leaves, is a perfect drought-tolerant annual for drier climates, such as Kansas City and other western Missouri cities, most summers. See www.savvygardener.com for a broader list of drought-tolerant plants. Kansas State University also adds the fluorescent-flowered Fairytales portulaca series to its list of top performers "for the climate and soils of the prairie" (www.prairiestarflowers.com). Check out also a new deep rose hybrid portulaca, 'Rio Scarlet'. It recently topped flower trials at the Missouri Botanical Garden.

Rudbeckia hirta, with its yellow daisylike petals and black brown centers, is commonly known as black-eyed Susan. It's a weed to some gardeners, a favored biennial wildflower—or short-lived perennial—to others. When plant geniuses got hold of it in recent years and hybridized the version 'Prairie Sun', they got a plant with spectacular 5-inch blooms, golden-yellow-tipped petals, and pale green central cones. It is the definition of "sun" as captured in a plant. It's a favorite of Jeff Oberhaus at Vintage Hill Farms. It won a 2003 top-flower award from All-America Selections (www.aaswinners.com).

Salvia coccinea 'Lady in Red' has been a favorite of Nikki Petitt's since she first planted it ten years ago in her Springfield garden. "It attracts hummingbirds better than other salvias," says the nursery manager for Wickman's Garden Village. "It reseeds itself freely without being invasive, and there's no deadheading or coddling." *S. coccinea* 'Coral Nymph'—with spikes of delicate rose, pink, and white flowers—shows up in another nearby yard and in online photos by Frank Shipe at www.ozarksgardens.com. "It would be hard to find a plant more pleasing in the garden than this sage we found in a rural west Greene County garden," he writes. Except, that is, for the tender perennial *S. guaranitica* 'Blue

Enigma'—a terrific hummingbird plant featuring cobalt blue tubular flowers. Garden centers also sell its gray blue brother, *S. guaranitica* 'Black and Blue'.

The New Kids on the Block

Calibrachoa, or million bells, is a group of tiny, petunia-like flowering annuals that took gardens by storm several years ago. "How did we get along without them?" many of container gardeners asked aloud. These plants trail beautifully over edges of pots. And when their flower colors of violet, blue, pink, red, magenta, yellow, or white got the addition of a terra-cotta hue, the *Calibrachoa* 'Sunbelkist' Million Bells Terra Cotta became an instant Plant of Merit at the Missouri Botanical Garden. New hues continue, such as 'Callie Purple Sunrise' and 'Callie Gold with Red Eye'.

Celosia plants may get put on display in your favorite local garden center before they start pushing up brushy red or yellow flowers. That's a good time to buy, however, because the plant is busier making roots than forcing blooms. It will bloom soon enough and long enough. And it may reseed with a vengeance. If you're looking at this plant for tufts of color in a container or garden bed, consider new cultivars, including *Celosia* 'Fresh Look Gold' and a gold-medal-winning 'Fresh Look Red', both from 2007 All-America Selections judging. Also, the new *C. argentea* 'Fresh Look Orange' made it on a recent Missouri Botanical Garden list of top-twenty picks from its flower trials.

Cuphea. A favorite version of this tropical "cigar plant" is *Cuphea* 'David Verity'. Hummingbirds can't stay away from the masses of small, orange, tubular flowers. And the dark green foliage alternates with the blooms, all on arching stems. The plant is prized by the Plants of Merit selectors for 2008 and among such nurserymen as Jeff Oberhaus of Vintage Hill Farms (www.vintagehill.com). Oberhaus also carries the new *C.* 'Flamenco Rhumba'—its many little flowers seeming to explode at their tips, making sense of its common name, firecracker plant. And the Missouri Botanical Garden's Kemper Center Annual Flower Trials give 'Flamenco Rhumba' top scores for heat tolerance, appearance, and flower production.

Diascia is another experiment gone right. Plant breeders made this native of temperate zones in South Africa somewhat more heat and humidity tolerant for use as an annual in the Midwest. Meanwhile, they've kept all of the charm of the original low-growing, richly flowering plant. Also called twinspur, this tender perennial produces pink or coral or apricot blossoms with yellow throats. Cultivars include 'Sun Chimes Coral' and 'Diamonte Apricot'. "Diascia planted in late March means you get three months of wonderful blooms," says Ricki Creamer, owner of Red Cedar Country Gardens (www.redcedargardens.com) in a Kansas City suburb. "And when it gets hot, you take it out or cut it back for the foliage."

Euphorbia 'Diamond Frost' is a new drought-tolerant, heat-tolerant landscape plant with masses of airy, white flowers on foot-tall plants. "It was probably the most asked about plant by the millions of visitors our gardens receive annually," writes a Smithsonian Institute staffer on the Web site of the national Proven Winners consortium of growers (www.provenwinners.com). Says Ann Lapedis of Sugar Creek Gardens in Kirkwood, "Customers who had it the first year raved about it. Apparently it really can take the heat and looks great with many different plants." A Plants of Merit committee agreed, adding it to the 2008 list.

Mexican petunia (*Ruellia brittoniana*) is a "thriller" of a plant, according to volunteer gardeners who plant median beds full of annuals in downtown St. Louis. The thrill comes from seeing deep purple, heat-and-humidity-resistant, petunia-like flowers on 3- to 4-foot stems, nodding above what the gardeners call "fillers"—or medium-height begonias and lantanas—and then "spillers," or trailing petunias. See the downtown plantings at www.gatewaygreening.org/UrbanRoots.asp.

Torenia fournieri is a revelation to newcomers. Also called wishbone flower, this striking, low-growing, warm-weather annual has small white blooms edged in dark blue—with stamens joined at the anthers, resembling a wishbone shape. New cultivars are *T.* 'Catalina Pink' and *T.* 'Summer Wave Amethyst'. In Missouri keep them in part shade and the soil uniformly moist to get best results in heat. "We grew this plant in pots on our deck last year for the first time," writes Joyce Cantrell of Mansfield, in her review on the Missouri Botanical Garden PlantFinder Web site. "It performed beautifully," she continues. "It is now a favorite."

Keeping Your Annuals Happy

Annuals newly planted in the ground need a regular soaking of water for the first month or so, while they get established, then a watering once a week with the inch or so given to the rest of the garden by sprinkler or other irrigation method. However, if the weather gets extremely hot and dry, check the soil with an index finger—an inch or so into the ground. If it's dry at that level, more watering is needed. And if you have annuals in containers, at least one watering a day in high heat is essential.

As for fertilizing, here's what Michelle Traub, head grower for Hillermann Nursery in Washington, recommends. Pot your annuals in Fertilome, Fafard, or some other professional potting mix. Either apply a Peters water-soluable 10-20-10 fertilizer once a week—especially if you're washing out the old fertilizer with daily waterings to beat the heat—or make sure you have time-release fertilizer worked into the soil. Organic fertilizers, such as Bradfield's Organics' 2-3-6 product made from alfalfa, molasses, sulfate

When to . . . *deadhead your annuals*

Every seven to ten days through the growing season. Dead-heading is important. It's how you initiate new flowering and keep your pots looking fresh. An alternative to deadheading is to fill your pots with new varieties, such as million bells (*Calibrachoa*), that take a bit more fertilizer but don't require the pinching of flowers. Wave petunias and 'Dragon Wing' begonias are "self-cleaning" in that sense, too.

of potash, and meat meal, are also available at Hillermann and at other Missouri garden centers. They are designed for vegetable beds but also work in containers with flowering annuals, just at a slower rate than do the synthetics.

Herbs, Vegetables, and Fruit

The interest in home-grown edibles has never been stronger, except perhaps in the era of victory gardens during World War II. Recent fears about food-supply contaminants are only a small part of the story. Missouri farmers' markets, specialty grocers, and a growing number of restaurants have hammered home the concept of food sourced locally and, often, from organic farms and gardens. Who wouldn't want to eat at a restaurant that includes on its menu "fresh homegrown oven roasted 'Red Ace' beets with orange-balsamic vinaigrette from Lee & Ingrid Abraham's Berger Bluff Farm in Berger, Missouri," or "homegrown Moscow Mills, Missouri, mint for mojitos tonight!" Those and other locally grown edibles are found seasonally at Riddles Penultimate Café in University City. Dining there and in other eateries with connections to local farms makes more than a few homeowners yearn to have little gardens of their own. And wait until they see the edibles growing in a new, innovative Heartland Harvest Garden—an extravaganza of good varieties for Missouri, planted on twelve of Powell Gardens' more than nine hundred acres near Kansas City. In opens to the public in spring 2009, around apple blossom time. Or at the new sixty-seven-acre Jefferson Farm and Gardens near Columbia, with grounds opening in late summer 2008.

Planning Your Edible Gardens

Wrap your mind around the concept of growing food at home. It's as simple as looking for the sunniest spaces in your yard and making sure that the soil is properly prepared.

Space. How much space will you need? That depends. Certainly not as much as the Powell or Jefferson Gardens have. Very little, in fact, if you are among a growing number of people who live where traditional gardening isn't possible but where growing herbs in containers on a deck or balcony is. Not so much space is needed for vegetables if your lettuces and tomatoes are pot planted in a good soilless mix and in full sun. Determinate tomatoes—ones that stop growing after reaching a compact size, from Totally Tomatoes (www.totallytomato.com), for instance—are perfect for container use. Certain fruits may take up little space if they are some of the newer dwarf varieties. There's even a way in spring to grow strawberries with no yard at all—in a freestanding, vertical patio kit from Missouri's own Stark Bro's Nurseries & Orchards Co. (www.starkbros.com).

Sunlight. If you have room and a hankering for a bigger edible garden, always look for a spot in full sun. That means six to eight hours of the strong light per day. Sun is a prerequisite for growing most annuals—a category for many vegetables and herbs in Missouri—so that they flower well and set fruit. But perennial food plants, including fruit trees and shrubs, also need full sun to develop flowers and then ripe fruit. And among other siting rules, every garden needs to be free from flooding, on level ground, in an open space that's not exposed to too much wind, and certainly not shaded by—or robbed of nutrients from—ornamental trees growing nearby.

A soil test for determining what structure and nutrients your plants need is best done through the University of Missouri Extension (see chapter 1). If you live in a long-populated urban environment and want to be doubly sure that heavy metals aren't in the food you grow, consider tests from the University of Massachusetts' specialized soil-testing lab (www.umass.edu/plsoils/soiltest). Vegetable gardeners in north St. Louis' New Roots Urban Farm make this Massachusetts connection each year to ensure that the produce they're selling to local restaurants and to subscription customers is as pristine as possible. See their work at www.newrootsurbanfarm.org.

Soil amendments. Based on soil-test results, amend with any nutrients found lacking and, just as important, with lots of organic matter—compost, peat moss, well-aged manure, or all three—tilled in for a loose, crumbly structure. This all implies that you've taken up sod and plan to plant directly in the ground, probably in Missouri's dense clay soil. There's no need to do that if you're willing to try a technique, newly called "lasagna gardening," the season before. This involves marking out the desired space for a new vegetable patch, allowing 2 feet for each row of plants and 2 to 3 feet for pathways between, and then layering, as you would noodles, cheese, and sauce for lasagna. Missouri master gardeners and others have long used the first layer—old newspapers—plus mulch for quick starts of garden beds on top of weeds or grass. Writer Patricia Lanza helped coin the phrase lasagna gardening for this process in the late 1990s. Generally, it starts with wetting newspaper pages and putting the damp paper in overlapping sections right on top of designated lawn. Pile on a 2-inch layer of peat moss, then compost, then composted manure, if you want, and more peat and compost—or even a layer each of grass clippings, garden soil, and chopped leaves. Your own personal recipe may dictate what's in the layers. A foot, even 2 feet, of material can build up. And it will eventually settle down to 6 or so inches of great soil. If layers are assembled in spring, remember that any manure that's used must be very well composted or it will burn the plants. Best results, however, come with a heavy lasagna approach in fall or winter, so that all layers and weeds have time to decompose and enrich native soil underneath.

Building Raised Beds

For many Missouri gardeners, the issue of raised beds in the garden all comes down to two techniques: mounding soil or enclosing soil.

Mounding soil. That's the very least that you should do, says Trish Grim of the fairly new north St. Louis subscription garden called New Roots Urban Farm. When she and a group of seven other young farmers got access to land owned by a neighborhood Catholic church, they built dozens of rows of 2-foot-tall mounded beds piled high with a mix of well-aged manure, compost, and top-soil that they had trucked in. Between these rows they hauled in mulch—enough to build it up nearly 2 feet so that the entire garden is practically level. But they top-dress and build up the gardened rows further each fall with compost that they make from their vegetable and flower leavings mixed with composted manure from the chickens that they keep. And they send off samples of the soil for testing each fall, just before top-dressing takes place.

Mounded garden beds have more square feet of soil exposed to sun than do flat, in-ground beds, and the raised ones warm up faster in the spring. The higher and fluffier the soil, the better the draining action is around roots.

Enclosing soil with planks, timbers, dry-stack rock, or inter-locking stones will form more structured raised beds. Don Schnieders of Jefferson City certainly does. Schnieders is retired from the excavating business that's still in his family, and he gardens full-time in what is arguably the best vegetable garden in Missouri. He has a medium-size, frost-free greenhouse for the seedlings that he's started very early in spring under lights in his basement. Many of these plants are donated to the Central Missouri Master Gardeners (extension.missouri.edu/cmregion/mg) for a popular spring plant sale. But most of them go into Schnieders's collection of wood-timber raised beds. Each is an unusual back-saving size of 3 feet tall, 20 feet long, and 5 feet wide, complete with drip tapes that have small emitters spaced 8 inches apart. "I can reach into and weed and harvest 2½ or 3 feet, easily," says this host of a weekly local-radio garden show. "I try to tell people that the secret to gardening is raised beds and drip irrigation," he adds. "The beds warm up a lot quicker in the spring, especially the tall raised beds." The dripping water goes only where it's needed, to each plant's roots. He gets tomatoes by June 15, Schnieders says, from soil that measures 10 degrees warmer in April than soil in the ground.

From Pots to Planks

The Pots to Planks program of the Missouri Botanical Garden takes donated plastic garden pots and recycles them into handsome black-plastic timbers for building raised beds, borders, or retaining walls. On weekends in May and June in St. Louis, volunteers and staff from the botanical garden accept most garden plastics—cell packs, trays, hanging baskets, and pots of all sizes—from homeowners and the horticulture industry alike. A special machine grinds the pots—some 100,000 pounds of them, one recent summer—for recycling into matte-black planks that are more like timbers. They are roughly the size of railroad ties, measuring 7 by 9 inches by 8½ feet long and each weighing 280 pounds. They sell for $40 each to those with appropriate load-bearing transportation, says a botanical garden spokesman. Proceeds go back to garden programs. For more information about plastic-pot recycling and the many collection sites in spring, go to www.mobot.org/hort/activ/plasticpots.shtml, or contact Steve Cline at steven.cline@mobot.org or (314) 577-9561.

Seven Tips for Organic Gardening Success

Gaylord Moore, recently retired horticulture specialist with the University of Missouri Extension office in Springfield, offers the following advice from his years of experience with vegetable gardening. His words come at a time when organic gardening, as a hobby, is growing in popularity alongside the awareness of food-safety issues and of climate change and other environmental concerns.

1. **Use and prepare organic matter to best benefit soil and plants.** Animal manures are excellent sources of organic matter and plant nutrients. Aged or composted manure may be applied spring or fall. When using fresh manure, it's always best to apply it in the fall and to incorporate it well into the soil. How much? Animal manures will vary in nitrogen amounts

depending on the animal source. Poultry manure is about 4.5 percent nitrogen, whereas cattle and horse manures are about 2 percent based on dry weight. Apply the equivalent of one-half to one pound of nitrogen per 1,000 square feet—or fifteen pounds of poultry manure per 1,000 square feet, or forty to fifty pounds of cattle manure to the same-size garden.

2. **Get soil tests to measure nutrients** and to help you decide what needs to be added to your soil. It's very important to be sure that the soil pH is acceptable for vegetables. Proper pH ensures that nutrients in soil are available to vegetable plants. Shooting for a pH of 6.5 is about right for most crops.

3. **Look for disease-resistant vegetable varieties** as the best way to reduce the chance of wilt, virus, powdery mildew, and the pests that attack weakened plants.

4. **Plant when soil temperatures are correct for maximum growth.** Check soil temperatures with a soil thermometer, easily found at garden centers or hardware stores. Ideal soil temperatures for most vegetables may be found in such publications as *Knott's Handbook for Vegetable Growers* (John Wiley & Sons). But crops also may be planted according to planting calendars. These are available through the University of Missouri Extension—see http://extension.missouri.edu/explore/agguides/hort/g06201.htm.

5. **Clean up weeds or other plants** that may serve as overwintering hosts, along with crop plants that have been diseased.

6. **Avoid introducing diseases.** Be certain that you buy healthy, disease-free transplants from your local garden centers or greenhouses. Avoid any plants that appear to be suspect—with spotting, wilting, or off color.

7. **Grow healthy plants to deter insects.** Natural and biological products are available for insect control. They include *Bacillus thuringiensis,* or Bt (sold as Dipel, Thuricide, and Biotrol). These are effective in controlling cabbage loopers and cabbage worms. Beneficial insects such as lady beetle larvae

and lacewings are good sources for helping to control aphids. Insecticidal soap, such as found in the Safer line of products, is often recommended for soft-bodied insects.

Deciding What to Grow

What a delicious decision-making process it is to pore through seed and plant catalogs and to walk the aisles of herbs and vegetables at favorite local nurseries, garden centers, and plant-society sales.

Herb Types, Varieties That Do Well in Missouri

Talk to experts around the state if you want to know what grows well in Missouri. Herbs that stand up to Missouri's climate and soils, for instance, are the perennial topic of Jim Long, an inveterate herb grower and author, at his company, Long Creek Herbs (www.longcreekherbs.com) in the delightfully named town of Blue Eye. According to an herb popularity survey that Long conducted recently for *The Herb Companion* magazine (www.herb companion.com), basil comes in a strong first on a list of top ten, with the rest following in this order: lavender, parsley, mint, rosemary, oregano, cilantro, thyme, sage, and chives.

But many other herbs have a following, too. "Herbs have been extremely popular for a number of years," says Long. "When the International Herb Association started in 1987, a lot of herb businesses also were getting started. I went to the first international conference thinking I was out there by myself," Long says of his small company. "And I walked in the door and, oh my gosh, there were two thousand people. It was almost like a happening, where everybody shows up at once." Nowadays, he adds, "there is an entirely new group of people coming along who are just discovering herbs."

Basil (*Ocimum basilicum*) is extremely popular among St. Louis herb gardeners, including the highly ornamental Thai basil, with purple stems and blossoms and hints of clove and mint in its flavor; 'African Blue' basil, a bushy energetic plant that may grow to 3 or 4 feet and render the warm, sweet scent of camphor; and that grocery-store staple, big-leafed 'Genovese Sweet' basil, with a slight, pleasing licorice taste. These only scratch the surface of basil-dom. Other basils found at a recent massive St. Louis Herb Society sale—see www.mobot.org/events for listings of this and other yearly plant-society sales—were 'Pesto Perpetuo', cinnamon basil, Red Rubin 'Purpurascens', and 'Napoletano Sweet'.

Lavender, second on the popularity list, is growing stronger in Missouri. Literally. An entrepreneurial couple, Steve and Deborah Nathe of Eureka, refused to listen to naysayers who told them that perennial lavender doesn't always come back in the humidity, poorly draining clay soils, and alternate freeze-thaw conditions of winter in the state. They decided to go ahead and sink money into a lavender business on a seventeen-acre family farm near St. Louis. Several years later, their Winding Brook Estate is a successful, cut-your-own operation and farmers'-market supplier. Here are just a few of their growing tips.

Besides making sure that lavender plants will be in full sun, the most important thing to do, the Nathes say, is to improve soil to a loose, fast-draining consistency. They add compost, sand, and pea gravel, mixed down into 18 inches of native soil. "The main problems with growing lavender in the central Midwest is the high summer humidity," they write on their Web site, www.windingbrookestate.com. "This sets the lavender up for fungal diseases. So don't crowd your plants; give them plenty of air circulation. We plant 3 feet apart." Soil tests are important, they say, as is adding a half cup of bonemeal and working it into each planting hole. "Lavender does not require and actually does better without heavy fertilizers and manures," they say. "If it doesn't rain each week, you will need to water your plant. But don't overwater. Lavender is drought tolerant once it is mature at three years old." Recently doing well at their farm were the lavender varieties 'Provence', 'Grosso', 'Seal', and 'Super'.

Parsley (*Petroselinum crispum*) is a biennial herb, meaning you'll find it treated as an annual in the garden center. But it may be grown from seeds that are soaked in water for a day or so before planting from early spring to late summer. Flat-leaf Italian parsley is a favorite for cooking, especially the variety 'Neapolitanum'.

Mint (*Mentha spicata*) is a perennial and so hardy that it may be invasive. Plant it in containers, even in plastic pots sunk into the garden, to keep it under control. 'Crispa' is a curly-leaf variety with spearmint flavor and flowers that butterflies adore.

Rosemary (*Rosmarinus officinalis*) is a tender, shrubby perennial that may or may not come back in parts of Missouri, depending on the winters. It scents the garden with a piney aroma and is quite drought tolerant. The rosemary cultivars 'Arp' and 'Hill Hardy' are said to be among the toughest.

Oregano (*Origanum vulgare* subspecies *hirtum*), or Greek oregano, is a perennial herb for Greek as well as Italian cooking. Seed companies also refer to it as *O. heracleoticum*. Either one is tasty and will tolerate dry soil.

Cilantro (*Coriandrum sativum*), or coriander, is an annual herb with a pungent flavor often added to both Mexican and Thai dishes. It is growing in popularity in Missouri. Baker Creek Heirloom Seeds of Mansfield offers not only a 'Slo-Bolt' variety but also new 'Oaxaca' seeds from Mexico.

Thyme (*Thymus vulgaris*) is a low-growing perennial that does well in Missouri, in part because of its need for humidity. 'Silver Posie' is a culinary thyme with tricolor leaves, making it ornamental as well.

Sage (*Salvia officinalis*) is a perennial herb with a woodsy, minty flavor that says "Thanksgiving" to many palates. In the garden it needs to dry out between waterings. 'Berggarten' is a popular cultivar.

Chives (*Allium schoenoprasum*) are hardy, clumping perennial plants with leaves imparting mild onion flavor. A few seedsmen

Garlic to Grow

A number of Missourians have taken to growing their own supplies of this biennial herb that's generally treated as an annual. Hardneck garlic (*Allium sativum*) is the type grown by Anne Cori of the St. Louis suburb called Ladue. She and her family prefer the 'German Red' variety. She also sells the harvested heads of this garlic in July at her cooking shop, Kitchen Conservatory (www.kitchenconservatory.com), in nearby Clayton. Search her blog for garlic news. Here's how their garlic garden grows.

They don't fuss with improving soil, since garlic is not particular. But they do plant it in their sunniest spot, on or about Columbus Day in mid-October, with the individual cloves of 'German Red'. Each clove is planted on a 1-foot center, with the root end down, so that the top of the clove is as deep as it is long. Straw covers the soil. Fertilizer is a basic 10-10-10 solution, and very little watering is done unless there's drought. In April each plant's scape, or emerging flower stalk, is cut to keep the plant's energy focused on developing the garlic head. Time to dig is when the plant's leaves start to wilt—around the Fourth of July. Harvested heads of garlic are kept dry, in a well-ventilated room. "But the day you dig the main crop, start eating it," says Cori, adding a one-word description of that experience—"delicious." To find other Missouri sources of garlic to garden with, try local farmers' markets, she says, or go online to search for gourmet garlic to grow in the garden. Grocery-store heads are often treated with sprout inhibitors, by the way, and are not good for planting at home.

sell the cultivar 'Windowsill Chives' developed for indoor growing.

Don't rule out indoor gardens—under lights or on sunny windowsills—with chives and several other herbs. To do this in winter, first look to such fall herb sales in Missouri as one each October by the Webster Groves Herb Society (www.wgherbs.org) and sponsored at Rolling Ridge Nursery (www.rollingridgenursery.com). Also, go to www.mobot.org/gardeninghelp/plantinfo.shtml and click on Kemper Factsheets and then Herbs for much more information on this topic.

Best Vegetables for Missouri

Tomatoes rule American vegetable gardens. And Missouri's are no different. In a tiny city backyard, so-called container tomatoes may be the way to go. But here are real, in-ground varieties—of tomatoes and of many other veggies—favored by experts around the state, including Don Schnieders, whose king-size home garden grows in Jefferson City; Gaylord Moore, retired extension specialist in Springfield; Trish Grim of New Roots Urban Farm in north St. Louis; Ben Sharda, executive director of the Kansas City Community Gardens; and Jere Gettle, in his own Mansfield garden, supplied by his Baker Creek Heirloom Seeds. And yet another broad list of what to plant is summed up in the excellent University of Missouri Extension guide called *Disease Prevention in Home Vegetable Gardens* found at http://extension.missouri.edu/xplor/agguides/hort/g06202.htm.

Tomatoes that top the charts in Missouri are the heirloom 'Cherokee Purple' for sweet flavor but not long shelf life. Eat them while you've got them. "I pick them just as soon as they start turning purple," says Don Schnieders. 'Cherokee Purple', says Gettle, "makes the best salsa I've ever had." Also grown by several of our experts is 'Brandywine', with beautiful, meaty pink fruit on indeterminate heirloom plants. Among the modern hybrids, 'Celebrity' is a tomato favored by those who also grow heirlooms. It has flavor, reliability, and, unlike some heirlooms, disease resistance. The medium-size tomato hybrid 'Jet Star' ranks high, too. "For reliability, it's hard to beat 'Jet Star'," says Sharda, whose group sells vegetable seeds to some two thousand low-income gardeners and others on a sliding scale based on income. "If that's the only tomato I could get, I'd be fine," Sharda adds. "'Jet Star' is just so reliable." 'Supersteak', meanwhile, is the beefsteak tomato of choice for Sharda, while 'Better Boy' is the large disease-resistant slicer that Gaylord Moore likes to grow. And 'Goliath' is a vigorous new hybrid producing golden yellow fruit for Schnieders. Another excellent MU guide—this one focused

Veggies in Containers

Go big—two gallons, for tomatoes—and use a professional, lightweight potting mix, never heavy soil dug from the garden. Good drainage from such mixes and air provided to roots is especially important in containers, since these relatively small structures create limited space for roots to thrive. Premier Pro Mix, Fafard, and Sunrise by SunGro Horticulture are just three professional mixes on the market. Or make your own soilless mix from equal amounts of peat moss and water-retaining minerals such as vermiculite or Perlite. Time-release fertilizer pellets may be mixed into the soil at planting time. Or a diluted version of the 10-10-10 soluable fertilizer used on annual flowers may be applied according to label instructions. Containers dry out more quickly than soil in the ground, so water daily to keep soil—especially for tomatoes—evenly moist.

only on growing tomatoes—is at http://extension.missouri.edu/
xplor/agguides/hort/g06461.htm.

Squash, of the yellow straightneck varieties, has cream-colored
fruit and more of it than the crookneck squash plants produce, says
Sharda. Gaylord Moore favors 'Dixie', 'Lemondrop', and 'Multipik'
squash varieties. And Jere Gettle says his heirloom 'Lemon Squash'
is resistant to squash borers while delivering excellent zucchini-like
flavor. Gettle, who knows that not all gardeners have the space to
grow vining squash plants, or indeterminate tomatoes for that matter, occasionally invites nationally known author Mel Bartholomew
to speak about space-saving gardening techniques at Gettle's heirloom seed festivals. And from a book and Web site called *Square Foot
Gardening* (www.squarefootgardening.com), Bartholomew brings
the idea of vertical netting to grow squash up, not out.

Peppers, to Gaylord Moore in Springfield, mean 'Merlin' and
'Paladin' as sweet peppers resistant to viruses and other disease.
Moore also likes to grow the medium-hot range of jalapeño peppers as well as the 'Hungarian Yellow Wax' pepper, the latter for
pickling, canning, and roasting. "My absolute favorite pepper,"
says Sharda, of Kansas City, "is the 'Gypsy' pepper hybrid. It's got
some 'Hungarian' heritage in it and starts out an elongated bell
and kind of lime green. But as you get farther into the season, it
gets a little more bell shaped and ripens to a butter yellow, then
orange, then red. Also, it's the earliest pepper I know of, and it
produces an incredible number of peppers per plant."

Random other vegetable choices include:

Beans. The choice is wide, from Gaylord Moore's 'Topcrop',
'Tendercrop', 'Kentucky Wonder', and 'Blue Lake' varieties to
'Chinese Red Noodle' beans favored by Jere Gettle with, he says,
"lots of deep red pods, about 18 inches long. They make a really
colorful sauté."

Cabbage. The 'Arrowhead' type (*Brassica oleracea*) that produces a narrow, elongated head is a favorite at New Roots Urban
Farm in north St. Louis because "the arrowhead shape means it

takes a lot less room to grow," says farm manager Trish Grim.

Carrots need loose, well-composted soil to develop properly. Varieties and carrot-planting times recommended by the University of Missouri Extension's Vegetable Planting Calendar— at http://extension.missouri.edu/explore/agguides/hort/g06201 .htm—include 'Amina', 'Bolero', 'Nantes Improved', 'Royal Chantenay', 'Sugarsnax 54', and 'Thumbelina'.

Cucumbers, the burpless varieties, meet their match in 'Japanese Long', a crisp, mild, easy-to-digest and good for Missouri version, sold as seed from Baker Creek Heirloom Seeds in Mansfield and at www.rareseeds.com.

Lettuce, that fairly hardy, cool-weather vegetable, to Ben Sharda means the spring variety called 'Canasta'. "It's not like a tight round head," he says, "but more of a looser head and crisp and more heat tolerant and more resistant to going to seed." Meanwhile, small heads of the romaine lettuce 'Red Sails' are what Don Schnieders plants in a raised bed along with 'Danvers Half-Long' carrots and radishes. With romaine he'll break off the tops to get regrowth. Otherwise, Schnieders harvests all three as they mature at different times—first radishes, then lettuce, and finally carrots as the others leave to make room.

Onions, especially green onions, were in the national news when contaminated ones showed up in certain restaurants and stores. Growing your own green onions from sets purchased at garden centers is a simple and rewarding task for home gardeners.

Watermelon that Jere Gettle "is really excited about," he says, is 'Royal Golden'—an heirloom with skin that first turns bright yellow and then golden yellow when ripe. The pinkish red flesh inside is crisp and sweet. This is a variety that was offered by an old Texas company, Wilhite Seed, and then dropped in the 1970s. But Gettle found it just in time for his 2007 seed catalog.

Fruits to Grow in Missouri

What are the most popular fruits for home gardens? That's the focus of a recent poll by the venerated Missouri grower Stark Bro's Nurseries & Orchards Co. (www.starkbros.com). And Stark Bro's got some surprising answers. Apples and peaches—the core of Stark's business—came in a bit lower on the scale than did smaller fruits sold by this historic company. Antioxidant-packed blueberries and dwarf cherries ruled.

Blueberries. Customers seem to love the 'Chandler' highbush blueberry (*Vaccinium corymbosum*), for instance. The native version of this highbush shrub grows in moist woods of the eastern United States. The 'Chandler' cultivar typically grows to between 5 and 6 feet, featuring, says the Missouri Botanical Garden's PlantFinder site (www.mobot.org/gardeninghelp/plantfinder), "perhaps the largest (cherry-size) blueberries produced by any highbush cultivar available in commerce today." In May the 'Chandler' fruits are preceded by lovely white, bell-shaped flowers.

A summary of good techniques for growing blueberries is mentioned on PlantFinder. But also look to exceptional advice on fruit growing from a program by Missouri State University at Mountain Grove. Go to http://mtngrv.missouristate.edu/MS-18/blueberry.htm, for instance, and find everything from blueberry "Spacing and Planting," "Pruning and Training," "Fertilizing," "Harvest," and more. Among the university's recommended cultivars is another highbush, *V. corymbosum* 'Blue Ray'. The botanical garden's PlantFinder concurs, saying that this blueberry shrub's "reddish stems have better winter color than those of most other blueberry varieties. 'Blue Ray' grows well in Missouri," the site concludes. Also visit the botanical garden's Kemper Center for Home Gardening to see planted versions of 'Chandler' and 'Blue Ray', as well as 'Atlantic', 'Blue Crop', 'Elliot', 'Herbert', 'Ivanhoe', 'Jersey', and 'Patriot'.

Dwarf cherries and other stone fruit—such as apricots— bloom so early in the spring that entire crops are lost when there's

Fruit-Tree Planting No-nos

- No weed-trimming power tools anywhere near the base of fruiting trees, or any tree for that matter. Injuries to the bark of a tree trunk destroy layers that conduct water and minerals from roots to leaves and that move food made by leaves to the rest of the tree.

- No pruning vacations. Pruning should be done once a year, in March, with removal of dead branches, crossover branches, and new vertical vegetation called water sprouts.

- No pests. Inexpensive tree-guard protectors that spiral around the trunk help prevent the eating of bark by rabbits at the base and by deer up above.

an unusually early cold snap. Still, polling by Stark Bro's finds that dwarf and semidwarf cherry trees are very popular for home gardeners with smaller yards. Planting them in protected sites is essential. One such cherry is the trademarked semidwarf Stark Montmorency Pie Cherry—what Stark calls "the most widely planted cherry in the United States." These trees—*Prunus cerasus*—are compact and produce fruit in mid-June. Another is Starkrimson Sweet (*P. avium* 'Lapins')—growing just to 12 or 14 feet tall, with fruit in late June. See the Missouri State University growing guide for recommended cultivars and cautionary tales at http://mtngrv.missouristate.edu/MS-18/stone.htm.

Peaches also may take a hit from early freezes. But they remain a sizable Missouri crop. The university's recommended peach varieties are 'Redhaven', 'Reliance', 'Glohaven', 'Summer Pearl,' 'Cresthaven', and 'Encore'.

Information on growing cherries, apricots, plums, pears, blueberries, and all manner of other berries also is found in the forty-page *Successful Planting and Growing Guide* supplied by Stark at the time of purchase or, in another form, via the University of Missouri Extension at http://extension.missouri.edu/explore/agguides/hort/#Fruit.

Apples. As for growing apples in Missouri, Elmer Kidd of Stark Bro's is the man to see. He's production director of the nearly two-hundred-year-old fruit-tree company, started when Kentucky pioneers settled on the west bank of the Mississippi River north of St. Louis in a town later called Louisiana, bringing with them a bundle of apple scions. From the resulting nursery came 'Red Delicious' and 'Golden Delicious' apples. Stark Bro's also sells everything from trees producing the grocery-store greats that are 'Gala' and 'Fuji' apples to such disease-resistant new cultivars as 'Enterprise' and 'GoldRush'.

"I rank apples as one of the hardest fruits to grow, relative to pests and diseases," Kidd says without hesitation. Interest in organic gardening may be as strong as ever, he adds. "But it's very hard to raise an apple to fruition without spraying it. You've got so many enemies on two sides of the spectrum. There are pests on one side of the teeter-totter, and on the other side, bacterial diseases." And so for new apple growers, there's a choice to be made. Don't spray and you don't get the most perfect-looking fruit, Kidd says. But there's hope in 'Enterprise', a firm red apple with crisp, spicy flavor and resistance to apple scab, cedar-apple rust, and fire blight. So, too, with the gold-colored 'GoldRush', also resistant to apple scab as well as powdery mildew.

When to . . . *plant fruit trees in Missouri*

Plant between late March and early May—as soon as the soil can be worked and air temperatures are still cool—for bare-root or balled-and-burlapped fruit trees. Or from November 1 to Thanksgiving, if bare-root trees are available.

Another way to look at apples in Missouri is from the perspective of the folks in charge of the new twelve-acre Heartland Harvest Garden at Powell Gardens, just east of Kansas City. Alan Branhagen, horticulture director at Powell, has relegated popular new 'Honeycrisp' apple trees to the interior of a spiral that is the garden's Apple Celebration Court, where fifty Missouri-grown fruit trees are arranged, with more vigorous ones planted on the outside of the spiral and less vigorous ones inside. "Newbies like 'Honeycrisp' are an international favorite but not fully tested here," Branhagen says. "I think star performers would be 'Jonathan', 'Golden Delicious', 'Starkspur Arkansas Black', 'September Wonder Fuji', and 'Red Delicious'." Best peach trees for the Heartland Harvest Garden, Branhagen says, are 'Redhaven', 'Burbank', 'July Elberta', 'Carolina Belle', and 'Starking Delicious'.

CHAPTER SIX

Natives

Homeowners around the country are more tuned in than ever to the value of native plants. "They are paying a lot more attention to environmentally friendly landscape options," says a recent summary of trends by leading members of the American Society of Landscape Architects, "such as adding native plants and managing storm water more effectively." In Missouri, native plants have been in vogue for years. Experts use them in drought-tolerant public plantings. A unique Grow Native! program that's a trademarked part of the Missouri Department of Conservation, in partnership with the state's Department of Agriculture, is nearly a decade old. And the number of Missouri home gardeners turning to natives as ornamentals is on the rise. Kansas City's 10,000 Rain Gardens initiative, meanwhile, is helping to fuel interest in natives that can take storm-water drenchings in quick-draining soils and then dry out completely for days, if not weeks. Even the legacy of the late Edgar Denison, a famous wildflower gardener and top-selling author from Kirkwood, continues to influence planters of natives inside and outside of the state.

What Is a "Native" Plant?

A Missouri native is a plant—flowering perennial, grass, tree, or shrub—that lived and reproduced long before settlers arrived, some say as far back as ten thousand years, in the clay, loam, and rocky soils found around the state. It defines Missouri in a most basic way. Native oak and hickory forests create canopies over large tracts of land in southern and eastern parts of the state, while tall grasses and wind-tossed flowers on sun-baked prairies gently roll to the north and west. Nearly all of these plants evolved to survive weeks without rain, only to endure the Midwest's occasional intense and soaking downpours. All the while they create homes and food sources for birds, butterflies, and other wildlife. For the home gardener the benefits are pretty clear: They are reliable sweeps of delicate native ground cover in shade, or masses of prairielike plants in sun, with wildlife nearly all year long.

"In round numbers, there are two thousand species of native plants in Missouri," says George Yatskievych, a man with credentials. He is a St. Louis–based botanist, president of the Missouri Native Plant Society, and director of the Flora of Missouri research project at the Missouri Botanical Garden. He also gardens with natives, especially with ferns—his all-time favorites for shade. But he adds that native plants aren't completely carefree. "You don't need to amend soil very much," Yatskievych says, "but growers of these plants do recommend mulch to keep down the competition from weeds. And natives do need some extra water the first year in the ground."

Are Natives Right for You?

There are at least two schools of thought on ways to use Missouri natives in the garden. There are the traditional gardeners who might mix a native or two in with their more manicured annual and perennial nonnatives—the latter plants also having higher water, fertilizer, and maintenance needs than natives do. Then there are the purists, who want all natives for more informal gardens that have low water needs; require only moderate mulching; and can flourish with no fertilizer, herbicides, or pesticides.

In between is someone like Judy Allmon, a pragmatic Jefferson City woman and founder of the state's Grow Native!

program. Allmon now consults on native plants and other gardening issues through her Bluestem Landscapes company (www.bluestemlandscapes.com). She sees both sides of this issue. "There's a nostalgic thing about old-fashioned wildflower gardens," says Allmon. "These plants won't necessarily stay put and behave like more familiar garden standards." Her advice when starting with natives is to "keep it simple. Don't try to have twenty different species in your butterfly garden, but instead plant a few species in masses of five or six plants each." And consider mixing natives with selections or cultivars of natives and other perennial plants. She does so on a little plateau high above Missouri River bottomland. This overlook—her backyard—features a serpentine border fronted with low-growing native crested iris (*Iris cristata*) plus the spikey white Appalachian native foamflower (*Tiarella cordifolia*). Then there are separate masses of at least two types of nonnative Shasta daisy hybrids, the white 'Becky' (*Leucanthemum* x *superbum*) and the yellow 'Broadway Lights' (*L. maximum* 'Leumayel'); clumps of native purple coneflower (*Echinacea purpurea*); hybrid daylilies; shrub roses; and the native Virginia sweetspire (*Itea virginica*), native winterberry (*Ilex verticillata*), and patented Coppertina ninebark (*Physocarpus opulifolius* 'Mindia')—a cultivar of the Missouri native with unusual exfoliating bark.

If you happen to live in the Missouri city of Creve Coeur, northwest of St. Louis, natives may be just right for you, but in a more controlled manner. That city recently amended its landscaping and weed ordinances to allow for natives, front and back, and to restrict the use of invasive plants. Specifically, it allows "orna-

Container Concepts

Natives can go into the smallest "gardens" ever. Author, garden designer, and television personality P. Allen Smith often includes U.S. natives in his container ideas at www.pallen smith.com. It's a way to get acquainted with these plants without making big in-ground commitments. For a Missouri readership, so does Alan Branhagen, director of horticulture at Powell Gardens near Kansas City. On the Web site of Critical Site's Prairie & Wetland Center—a native-plant supplier—Branhagen writes about low-cost ways of trying out natives in pots. Consider his "Summer Prairie-esque" planting, starting with a large, weatherproof container, approximately 24 or 36 inches in diameter, with an opening to allow for drainage and good container soil that's kept evenly moist but not wet. He plants a centerpiece of the grass prairie dropseed (*Sporobolus heterolepis*); three blooming pale purple coneflowers (*Echinacea pallida*) spaced around the centerpiece; three prairie onion plants (*Allium stellatum*), one each between the coneflowers; small plants of 'Silver Blade' primrose— the everblooming selection of Missouri primrose (*Oenothera macrocarpa* subspecies *incana* 'Silver Blade')—and purple poppy mallow (*Callirhoe involucrata*), tucked in around the edges to spill over. For Branhagen's complete article on natives in containers, go to www.critsite.com, click on Resources and then Signature Landscapes.

mental grasses and native plants taller than 7 inches. Certain exclusions exist, for example, the plants cannot obstruct sight distances and must have 5-foot setbacks from neighboring properties." The ordinance continues: "Native plants have been shown to reduce maintenance and effectively conserve water, soil, and other elements of the natural community. Moreover, the preservation, restoration, and management of native plant communities reduces the need for toxic pesticides, herbicides, fertilizers, and other pollutants into the environment." Says Fran Cantor, chair of the city's Recycling, Environment, and Beautification committee at the time of the ordinance's passage, "The bottom line is, it's one of the things we can do to help repair the world. We harm the environment in so many ways, and native plants repair some of the damage."

That's what folks at Shaw Nature Reserve, located in Gray Summit, think, too. Shaw, a division of the Missouri Botanical Garden, has a new Native Plant School that instructs—in three-hour classes held mostly outdoors and year-round—on the topics of native home landscaping as well as on prairie, savanna, and wetland establishment. It uses its naturally designed, intensely planted Whitmire Wildflower Garden as a teaching tool. More than eight hundred Missouri native species grow there. See what Shaw has to offer at www.shawnature.org.

Matching Natives to the Site

The following are a few examples of what to plant where in your native garden. Besides getting help from a native landscaping guide on the Shaw Nature Reserve Web site (www.shawnature .org), check out extensive lists of natives and their cultures on the Grow Native! site (www.grownative.org) and on Critical Site's www.critsite.com. (For native trees, see chapter 8.)

Flowering Natives for Mostly Dry Sites

These are the grasses, asters, coneflowers, and others that you might think of as prairie plants, but more:

Aromatic aster (*Aster oblongifolius*) is a sun-loving plant for blooms in the fall, a goal that gardeners sometimes overlook. This aster is a much more compact plant—around 2 feet tall—than the common roadside plant and is covered in August and September with blue purple daisylike flowers and scented leaves. It prefers well-drained to dry soil and is on the emeritus listing of Missouri's Plants of Merit.

Fragrant sumac (*Rhus aromatica*) is a larger (2 to 6 feet tall), shrubbier, and equally fragrant native that likes full sun or part shade. Its yellow green flowers appear in early spring, followed by aromatic leaves, then red fruit on female plants starting in late summer, and then fall leaf colors of yellow, orange, and purple. Some Missouri landscapers are beginning to use the more compact and dense *R. aromatica* cultivar 'Gro Low' as an excellent, low-mounded ground cover. Fragrant sumac is a Plant of Merit emeritus.

Gray-head coneflower (*Ratibida pinnata*) actually has large yellow flowers with drooping petals surrounding brown seed heads. It blooms all summer in full sun and dry conditions. It also does well in clay. The best look for this plant in ornamental gardens is as massed plantings, although be aware that it tends to self-seed and spread.

Little bluestem (*Schizachyrium scoparium*) is a small, non-spreading grass with blue green leaves that grow in pleasing mounded clumps. Leaves turn reddish orange in fall, and silver seed heads last through winter. It takes full sun, dry to average soil, and easily tolerates Missouri's heat and humidity.

Missouri evening primrose (*Oenothera macrocarpa*) features large, yellow, fragrant flowers—up to 4 inches across—on foot-tall plants. Bloomtime lasts from spring through summer. This native grows well in poor soil, even during drought, but needs full sun and good drainage.

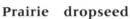

Prairie blazing star (*Liatris pycnostachya*) will take dry conditions—even drought—but also thrives in more moist, well-drained soils. Its 2- to 4-foot-tall flower stalks in July and August are a pale lilac hue. Butterflies and hummingbirds like this plant's nectar, and songbirds go for its seed. It is somewhat intolerant of wet soil in winter.

Prairie dropseed (*Sporobolus heterolepis*) is a drought-tolerant, tough, as well as pretty little grass, featuring thin green leaves that form a thick clump of arching shapes, with aromatic seed heads in late summer. It thrives in full sun. Clumps turn deep orange in fall. It is a Plant of Merit.

Purple beardtongue (*Penstemon cobaea*) has June-blooming tubular flowers in show-stopping shades of violet and purple, all on 1- to 2-foot stalks. It needs full sun and dry, well-drained soil.

Wild bergamot (*Monarda fistulosa*) is a sun-loving native with lavender pink whorl-like flowers and a long bloom period in summer. It grows between 2 and 4 feet tall and needs air circulation to prevent powdery mildew. Its soil needs are dry to medium moist and well draining.

Flowering Natives for Moist Sites

Here are just a few of many plants for moist, shady woodland conditions or in sun for the edges of ponds:

Blue false indigo (*Baptisia australis*) is a bit of a crossover plant, needing medium-wet soil to get established but tolerating dry conditions, even drought, once mature. Full sun is needed for the best blooming of cobalt blue clusters of flowers in spring on this shrublike native. A sister plant is the white false indigo (*B. alba*).

Celandine poppy (*Stylophorum diphyllum*) is a shade-loving, early-spring bloomer with delicate poppylike yellow flowers and large, lobed leaves. It grows best in moist soil and will go dormant in summer without it.

Purple coneflower (*Echinacea purpurea*) is the classic crossover plant—prairie and home garden, needing medium-wet, well-drained soil in full sun for large pinkish purple, daisylike blooms that butterflies love June through August.

Virginia bluebells (*Mertensia virginica*) produce pink buds in March that open in clusters of blue bells in April. Foliage is blue green. This plant is a spring ephemeral, meaning the foliage goes dormant in summer. Great for naturalizing in a rich, moist woodland environment.

Outright Rain Garden Plants

If you're inspired by Kansas City's 10,000 Rain Gardens initiative (www.rainkc.com), you might want to try a small rain garden near a downspout, a driveway, or another low point that collects water in your yard. Rain gardens are shallow, flat-bottomed swales—each about 6 to 12 inches deep and planted with garden-worthy natives that have deep roots to help channel water as it filters through soil deeply into the ground. Before installing a rain garden, check with your utility for the location of any underground pipes or lines, then try a percolation test, making sure that your soil drains well enough to eliminate any chance of ponding and hosting mosquitoes. Dig a coffee-can-size hole where you think the rain garden would be deepest. Fill the hole with water, mark the water level, and measure the drainage difference after four hours. If water falls 1 inch in that time, say the experts, it will percolate 6 inches in twenty-four hours. And that's the deepest that your rain garden should be.

Ferns Are Natives, Too

Native ferns grow in the St. Louis garden of George Yatskievych, the botanist and native-plant expert who also is membership secretary of the American Fern Society. Here is his list of the shade-loving plants:

Cinnamon fern (*Osmunda cinnamomea*), a Missouri native that grows to 3 feet tall, with glossy pale green fronds in spring, becoming cinnamon-colored in the fall. It prefers moist soil but will adapt to dryer conditions.

Christmas fern (*Polystichum acrostichoides*), a Plant of Merit, an evergreen, and a Missouri native, with dark green lance-shaped fronds growing to about 30 inches.

Maidenhair fern (*Adiantum pedatum*), with finely textured soft green fronds and dark stems, growing from 10 to 18 inches tall. It is a Missouri native and a delicate addition to shady spaces, needing water when conditions are dry.

Ostrich fern (*Matteuccia struthiopteris*), with broad, medium green fronds that may grow as tall as 4 feet. This Missouri native makes an excellent background for shade gardens. It prefers damp, rich soil.

Royal fern (*Osmunda regalis*), a large graceful fern with broad fronds that have well-separated leaflets and yellow fall color. It will grow in wet ground.

Sensitive fern (*Onoclea sensibilis*), a native to the Eastern United States. This 3- to 4-foot-tall fern with light green, deeply lobed fronds is called sensitive because it needs consistently moist soil. It dies back after a first frost in fall.

Here are just a few of the wet-soil natives to consider:

Blue lobelia (*Lobelia siphilitica*) does not tolerate drought. In fact, it needs constant moisture in full sun or part shade. And in September and October, it forms spectacular, blue two-lipped flowers on 2- to 3-foot stalks.

Cardinal flower (*Lobelia cardinalis*) produces scarlet red blooms that hummingbirds love on 2- to 4-foot stalks from July to September. It is happiest in rich, wet soil. It is an emeritus Plant of Merit.

Fox sedge (*Carex vulpinoidea*) grows in clumps and in wet conditions, at the very edge of water. It has narrow leaf blades up to 3 feet tall and seed heads in fall that spray from the center of the plant.

Marsh milkweed (*Asclepias incarnata*) may grow 4 or 5 feet, with tufts of white, pink, or mauve blossoms in July and August. It is a food source for the monarch butterfly and needs wet soils to flourish.

Soft rush (*Juncus effusus*), also called corkscrew rush, grows in saturated to wet conditions, sending up stiff, slender leaves, 20 to 40 inches tall, in attractive clumps that do well pondside or in consistently moist home gardens. In Missouri clumps die to the ground in winter.

Maintenance of Natives?

There is no no-maintenance landscape. But you can come close, says Scott Woodbury of Shaw Nature Reserve, if you choose the right natives to plant. You generally don't have to fertilize, mulch,

When to . . . *go native*

Spring is the best time, in part, because that's when there are native-plant sales around the state. Here are a few:

- Mother's Day weekend is the time for an extensive annual sale sponsored by Shaw Nature Reserve and featuring vendors across Missouri. Shaw is located about 35 miles west of St. Louis on Interstate 44 at Gray Summit. For more information on the sale or other native-plant events, go to www.shawnature.org.

- The first weekend in May is when Powell Gardens features its Spring Festival and Plant Sale. Usually Missouri Wildflowers Nursery (www.mowildflowers.net), based in Jefferson City, takes part. Powell is located about 40 miles southeast of Kansas City, near Kingsville, on U.S. Highway 50. Go to www.powellgardens.org for more information.

- Year-round a new Missouri Exchange Web site (www.missouriexchange.com) is a virtual matchmaking system that hooks up native-plant seed producers and growers with buyers. The University of Missouri Center for Agroforestry, in cooperation with the Grow Native! program, started this online marketplace in January 2007 "to increase business opportunities for native plants, materials, and Missouri alternative products." It also may help struggling small farmers create extra income. Registration is free. E-mail a message to webmaster@missouriexchange .com; mail your questions to the University of Missouri Center for Agroforestry, Missouri Exchange Online Marketplace, 203 A.B.N.R. Building, Columbia, MO 65211; or phone (573) 882-4848.

or water native plantings, once they're established. But if you go the native route, he says, you can expect some surprises, such as new seedlings of your natives popping up in unexpected parts of the garden or occasional wilting of a plant during drought. And generally with natives your garden will look more informal and natural than with cultivated varieties. On the other hand, if you chose a more manicured planting style, he says, you'll need to water more, mulch more, and generally maintain the garden more to keep competition from weeds at bay. Whatever your garden approach, natives do need regular watering and some mulching during their first season of growth.

CHAPTER SEVEN

Perennials and Bulbs

Hardy perennials and bulbs for Missouri are long-lived plants that tolerate winters, bloom reliably in summer, and make many of our gardening chores a whole lot easier. They're still popular these days, even though it's been years since the perennial surge of the 1980s and '90s—when breeders and garden centers alike jumped on the enthusiasm of baby boomers who were starting to use perennials as foundations for new home gardens. Tropicals, flowering shrubs, and annuals may be grabbing new interest, but anticipation and fanfare still greet the introduction each year of new perennial hybrids. For proof you only have to look at the dozens of new-hued and -shaped cultivars of wild coneflower— purple *Echinacea purpurea* and yellow *E. paradoxa*. Newest may be a double called *E.* 'Coconut Lime' or one of the darkest oranges in *E.* 'Tiki Torch'. Watch your local garden center for more.

"What's so great about perennials?" says Ricki Creamer, owner of the Kansas City area's Red Cedar Country Gardens (www.redcedargardens.com), as she responds to a tongue-in-cheek question. "I like perennials for their varied textures and colors of leaves. You can't find these differences in annuals as much. I am fond of the seasons of bloom, from spring to winter, and fall especially here because it's so long and we have great color from perennials at that time. Also, the transition of height from tree to shrub to perennial is a good one. And I adore the different shapes of bloom. Yes, there is maintenance. But my own perennial garden has been planted for ten years with just a tiny bit of division and it is still going strong."

Plan a Perennial Garden

Home gardeners turn to perennials not only for the flowers and foliage but also for attracting birds and butterflies, for scenting the space, and for keeping bare ground covered and in place.

By Theme

Butterfly gardening. One of the most popular gardening themes—for sun-drenched spaces—is a perennial bed built for attracting butterflies and birds. And there's no better such garden in the St. Louis area than one by a guy who calls himself Tom Terrific. He is Tom Krauska of Crestwood. Under the Tom Terrific moniker, he's turned a passion for observing, feeding, and providing perennial homes for butterflies and other pollinators into an occupation. He speaks on the subject to everyone from grade school children to nurserymen to gardeners at seminars. He produces e-zines, Web sites, photos, books, and videos. See just a little of his work at www.butterflygardening.org. And while you're there, look at his list of two-hundred-plus plants trialed in his own garden. His "notes" include positive reviews as well as helpful critiques, such as "invasive," "leggy," "expensive," and "pretty flower, but few butterflies."

Scenting the scene is increasingly important to home gardeners. Why install a pretty flowering plant that has no scent when you can get flowers and fragrance all in one? Think of *Echinacea* 'Twilight', says Alice Longfellow, owner of Longfellow's Garden Center in Centertown (www.longfellowsgarden.com). The plant has an unexpected sweet scent as well as dark pink blooms on tall, sturdy stems. Its peach-colored cousin, 'Matthew Saul', also is from the trademarked Big Sky series of echinaceas

Tom Terrific's Top Ten . . .

These are Tom's picks of perennials for sunny, Missouri butterfly gardens. See more at www.butterflygardening.org.

Bronze fennel (*Foeniculum vulgare*). 'Smokey' is an attractive cultivar. It draws the black swallowtail butterflies that use it as a home for larvae.

Butterfly bush (*Buddleia davidii*). "The best overall nectar bush," he writes in notes on his Web site.

Butterfly weed (*Asclepias tuberosa*) is a monarch magnet. "Great plant!" he writes.

Eastern blazing star (*Liatris scariosa*), an "excellent September bloomer; monarchs love it."

New England aster (*Aster novae-angliae*), a Missouri native and host plant for pearl crescent butterflies. "The best fall nectar plant."

Pearly everlasting (*Anaphalis margaritacea*) attracts painted and American lady butterflies. "Excellent host plant in spring, plus pretty flowers in the fall."

Purple coneflower (*Echinacea purpurea*), in new cultivars as well as the straight species that's a Missouri native, are flowers that butterflies love. And birds like the seeds in fall.

Shasta daisy (*Leucanthemum* x *superbum*), especially the 'Becky' cultivar, is "an excellent bloomer," says Krauska. The Perennial Plant Association likes it, too, making it the top choice for 2003.

Slender mountain mint (*Pycnanthemum tenuifolium*), with 1- to 3-foot-tall stems ending in small, flat, white flowers that are attractive to bees, butterflies, and skippers.

Speedwell (*Veronica* 'Sunny Border Blue'), a striking plant for full sun, with 2-foot-tall spikes packed with dark blue flowers. *V. spicata* 'Royal Candles' is another great option.

bred by Richard Saul of www.itsaulplants.com and is almost a rose-scent sweet. Or there's the fragrant daylily *Hemerocallis* 'Siloam Cinderella', Longfellow says, with cream and pale pink flowers that emit a mild, pleasant aroma. Even the low-growing native perennial evening primrose (*Oenothera macrocarpa*) has a pleasing scent to its large yellow blossoms. When in doubt, go to the Missouri Botanical Garden's PlantFinder site (www.mobot .org/gardeninghelp/plantfinder) and look for such phrases as "has fragrant flowers" and "leaves are fragrant."

Covering ground is another theme of sorts, one pursued by Arlie Tempel of Ferguson, who uses hostas to great effect in his shady, sloping backyard. But his slopes are extreme—as much as 30 degrees in spots. Lawn would be difficult, if not impossible. After shade from mature trees took over his once sunny space, he began planting, dividing, and planting more hostas. In summer in Tempel's nearly one-acre yard, this extremely reliable perennial for Missouri—representing some eighty varieties for collector Tempel—becomes a massive green ground cover. When the St. Louis Hosta Society hosts the American Hosta Society's national convention, Tempel's garden is on the tour. "We started small eighteen years ago," Tempel says, "planting hostas close to the house. And then, as one gentleman said many years ago, 'We all did daylilies until we started having shade in our garden and then switched over to hostas.'"

Keeping Your Plants Happy

Perennials need the right place to thrive—sun or shade, depending on the plant; good soil; water; nutrients; and occasional division to boost plant health and to increase plant numbers.

Sun Versus Shade

A good plant tag tells the story with a symbol: first, full sun and a sun-filled circle for a plant that loves six or more hours of the hot stuff each day; then part sun/part shade and a half-black circle for plants that take only six hours or less of sun, preferring afternoon shade; then shade and an all-black circle for those plants that thrive under trees or in other shade. Shade plants, by the way, often have larger, thinner leaves—think hostas—that may be more efficient at harvesting sunlight at lower levels of light. In sunlight that's too intense, these shade leaves overload and may look burnt. Siting is key. Watch this space—meaning the space that's your yard—and choose plants based on the light conditions there.

Soil Amendments

Preparing soil is crucial. Turn peat, compost, and even well-aged manure into new garden beds, even mound those beds with generous amounts of the mix for especially good drainage. Drainage for bulbs is essential. (See chapter 1 for more details.)

Watering and Fertilizing

A good 1½ inches of water per week—either from irrigation or rain—may be measured with an inexpensive rain gauge. Such thorough weekly waterings help roots go deeper for the water that seeps downward. And deeper roots give plants a better chance to survive dry periods. As for fertilizing, moderation again is key. Suitable ratios of soluble, or granular, synthetic fertilizers in the first year after planting may be a balanced 10-10-10 (equal percentages of nitrogen, phosphorus, and potassium), or 10-20-20 for more phosphorus that helps build strong root systems and potassium for flowering and fruit. Too much nitrogen promotes excessive vegetative growth. However, I and some other perennial gardeners often cut the rate of these fertilizers in half and apply them twice a month in that first summer, rather than giving the plants a month's worth of nutrients all at once. Another option is to use a nine-month, slow-release fertilizer with a ratio of 18-6-12, with the first number—nitrogen—triple-coated for slowest release. Schultz MultiCote 18-6-12 Time-Release Plant Food is one such product, Osmocote 18-6-12 is another. And gardeners looking for low-maintenance perennials may, in subsequent years, fertilize only once a year, a few weeks before flowering.

Interest in organic growing of flowering perennials also is on the rise. This means applications of compost and/or well-rotted manures for top-dressing existing beds. This is a slower way to fertilize—with fewer nutrients, weight for weight—but more satisfying for folks interested in long-term improvement of soils and plants. And at least one Missouri company, Bradfield Organics, is part of the Land O'Lakes Purina Feed group that's manufacturing an organic product of alfalfa, molasses, sulfate of potash, and meat meal with a 3-1-5 NPK ratio for gardens, as well as others for vegetables and lawn. For information write to Feed Solutions, P.O. Box 66812, St. Louis, MO 63166; call (800) 551-9564; or visit www.bradfieldorganics.com. The Web site lists nearly fifty Missouri garden centers selling its products.

Dividing

Dividing is the no-cost way to increase plant numbers while improving the health of overgrown perennials. With pitchfork in hand, and in dry conditions, dig up the root-ball, crown, and foliage of a plant. Then divide portions of the perennial into pieces by pulling them apart, making sure that each division keeps a small root system plus two or more shoots. Replant these in or around the garden. Kansas City's online gardening guide, www.savvygardener.com, has an especially helpful listing of when, how often, and exactly how to divide specific perennials. And in St. Louis a substantial springtime event called the Great Perennial Divide is a charitable event of sorts, helping gardeners "dispose" of divisions by getting them to community gardens around the city. The Great Perennial Divide is sponsored by the not-for-profit Gateway Greening, Inc. (www.gatewaygreening .org; click on Upcoming Events) and also features a spring plant sale with proceeds going to community-gardening projects.

Best Perennials for Missouri

There are many great perennials for our state. Here the list has been culled to appeal to the range of temperatures and other conditions across the state—with USDA Cold Hardiness Zone 5 or colder a prerequisite. You may freely experiment with Zone 6 in protected spots. Or as climates change and grow warmer, Zone 7 plants may even be an option not only in southern but also in central parts of the state or, again, tucked into ultraprotected parts of your yards.

A word or two of advice on perennials: Names can be confusing. For example, some Latin names have been changed, not to protect the innocent—as the old TV crime shows maintained—but to satisfy the needs of botanists and other plant experts. The most striking example is the genus *Chrysanthemum*. It's been divided into *Dendranthema* for showy garden mums—although *Chrysanthemum* still is used for them in some garden centers—and into *Leucanthemum* for Shasta daisies. Meanwhile, more than a few annuals and perennials share common names, such as the annual plumbago (*Plumbago capensis*), producing gorgeous, powder blue phloxlike blooms on 3-foot stems, and the hardy, low-growing perennial plumbago (*Ceratostigma plumbaginoides*), with tiny dark blue flowers every year that have won it a Missouri Plant of Merit honor. When in doubt, look up plants on the Missouri Botanical Garden's PlantFinder site at www.mobot.org/gardeninghelp/plantfinder.

Old favorites are new again. And newcomers are welcome additions to most perennial beds. Here are just a few:

Bleeding heart (*Dicentra spectabilis*) is an import from the Far East. This one is shade loving in the heat of Missouri summers, toward the end of which it goes dormant and gets covered by foliage from hostas, ferns, or other later-leafing plants. But in spring this longtime garden favorite produces arching stems covered in the most beautiful white-petaled flowers that, in turn, are partly covered with pink, heart-shaped outer petals. New varieties of old-fashioned bleeding heart may be found at, among other Missouri sources, Sugar Creek Gardens in Kirkwood (www.sugarcreekgardens.com), including all-white hearts on the stems of *D. spectabilis* 'Alba'; gold foliage on *D. spectabilis* 'Gold Heart'; and dark-rose-colored flowers over blue green foliage in 'Candy Hearts'. And for a species cousin, take a look at *D. formosa* 'King of Hearts', with rosy pink heart-shaped flowers in spring and summer.

Catmint (*Nepeta racemosa*) is an alternative to lavender for Missourians who've given up on growing that pale lilac herb in difficult weather and soils. And the *Nepeta* cultivar 'Walker's Low' became the 2007 Perennial Plant of the Year for its foot-tall, lavender-hued blooms from June through September and its attractive gray green foliage. See www.perennialplant.org for details. For borders consider the more compact new *N.* 'Kit Kat'. For bigger impact there's the 3-foot-tall *N.* 'Six Hills Giant'. In between is the Plant of Merit catmint *N. racemosa* 'Blue Wonder'—one that thrives in full sun and is very drought tolerant. Alice Longfellow of Longfellow's Garden Center (www.longfellowsgarden.com) likes catmints for several reasons, including "that they fit that Mediterranean, Tuscan color scheme that's very popular. We also do tend to be very dry," she says of her central Missouri location.

Coralbells (*Heuchera micrantha*) made a splash in shady home gardens in 1991 when the new reddish bronze leaves of *H.* 'Palace Purple' helped make it the Perennial Plant of the Year. Members of the Perennial Plant Association select from thousands of plants for beauty, easy care, and suitability to a wide range of climates. Other folks value new heucheras, too. "Few perennials have undergone as dramatic a makeover as heucheras (coralbells) and their hybrids with tiarellas (foamflowers), the heucherellas (foamy bells)," says the publisher Timber Press of a 2005 garden classic, *Heucheras and Heucherellas*, by Dan Heims. Relatively new is a heuchera with bright peach-colored leaves—'Peach Flambé'—

a favorite at Vintage Hill Farms in Franklin (www.vintagehill.com) as well as at Greenscape Gardens in Ballwin (www.greenscape gardens.com). *H.* 'Southern Comfort' is new, too, and a favorite of Idyllwild Gardens in Savannah (www.idyllwildgardens.com) for its 8-inch leaves of a burnished-copper color that are bred to take Missouri's heat as well as its winter cold. And don't forget about the "bells" in this plant's common name, specifically clusters of lit-tle bells in a deep scarlet hue in such plants as *H. sanguinea* 'Ruby Bells'—often found at Wall Flowers Nursery in New Bloomfield.

Daylily (*Hemerocallis* species) is a sun-loving perennial that's at or near the top of any roster of dry-weather plants. See the list of "Drought-Tolerant Flowers for the Kansas City Metro Area" on the Web site www.savvygardener.com. And think of the daylilies in your Grandma's country garden, with showy orange or yellow flowers that come and go each day and rarely need care. Nowadays such Missouri growers as Chris Schaul at Wine Country Gardens in Defiance (www.winecountrygardens.net)

feature hundreds of new daylily varieties. Top sellers for Schaul are the pale pink 'Barbara Mitchell', the large red and yellow spider form 'Firestorm', golden orange double 'Prester John', and the tiny yellow 'Bitsy'. Dwarf, repeat-blooming daylilies are especially popular in the Missouri landscape, Schaul says. Golden 'Stella de Oro' got things started in the 1980s and '90s and now, some say, is overused. But there's also the lemon yellow 'Happy Returns' and purple 'Always Afternoon'. Speaking of late-day, scorching Missouri sun, says Schaul, "it behooves people to put daylilies in afternoon shade if they want them to stay looking nice." Also check out one of the oldest daylily sources in the state—Gilbert H. Wild & Son of Sarcoxie (www.gilberthwild.com).

Epimedium 'Creeping Yellow' is so new it may not even be at your neighborhood garden center. And yet it is a very striking version of that distinctive, low-growing ground cover with heart-shaped leaves ideal for shade and dry sites. It was launched in Great Britain and would certainly add the look of sunlight under a dense canopy. Or look for the widely available *E.* x *versicolor* 'Sulphureum', with green heart-shaped leaves that are tinged with red in spring and that turn all red in fall.

Feather reed grass, specifically *Calamagrostis* x *acutiflora* 'Karl Foerster' is a delightfully tall and wispy addition of ornamental grass to garden beds. Its verticality—at 3 to 5 feet—and slowness to spread, plus golden tan color in fall, helped make it Perennial Plant of the Year (www.perennialplant.org) in 2001. It's also on the emeritus list of Plants of Merit (www.plantsofmerit.org). Want something a little smaller? Consider *C.* x *acutiflora* 'Overdam', a variegated reed grass that grows 2½ to 3 feet, will take some shade, and—like 'Karl Foerster' and unlike many other ornamental grasses—thrives in clay soils. Its purple blooms companion nicely with the dark purple of *Salvia nemorosa* 'Caradonna' (see below).

Geranium, of the winter-hardy type, is gaining ground in Missouri home gardens. Exceptional heat tolerance and the delicate, summerlong, blue violet blooms of *Geranium* 'Rozanne' are two reasons why. It was discovered in England in the early 1990s and came to U.S. gardens shortly thereafter. Its appeal is subtle, with mounds growing only to about 1 foot and spreading in and around other taller plants. But it quickly became a Plant of Merit and a favorite with such retailers as Garden Heights Nursery in Richmond Heights (www.gardenheights.com) and at Soil Service Nursery in Kansas City. A Perennial Plant of the Year for 2008, it now has its own Web site—www.geraniumrozanne.com. Also watch out for newer sister plants, such as one with bronze foliage and bright pink flowers called 'Orkney Cherry' or another with black-centered magenta flowers called 'Perfect Storm'. *G.* 'Pink Penny', the violet 'Jolly Bee', or the lavender blue 'Sweet Heidy' are just a few others in this explosive category.

Hosta is a genus of plants that are made for shade under the mature trees of Missouri. In cooler climates these leafy perennials may even withstand noonday summer sun. But when Missouri cranks into 90-degree heat in July and August, hostas need shade as well as consistently moist soil. The 2-foot-tall and -wide cultivar 'June' has gold and blue green variegated leaves that have made it a Missouri Plant of Merit emeritus. But Ronna Moore of Idyllwild Gardens in Savannah likes the even brighter gold foliage with blue green borders of 'Paradigm', also bigger at about 3 feet tall and wide. It was

Hosta of the Year in 2007, as chosen by the American Hosta Growers Association (www.hostagrowers.org). Moore also favors 'Stained Glass', a 2006 Hosta of the Year with even more gold to each leaf. The 2008 choice is the charming, small all–blue green 'Blue Mouse Ears', while 2009's Hosta of the Year is a variegation of a different kind—creamy white edges to blue leaves of the five-foot-wide 'Earth Angel'.

Japanese anemone (*Anemone* x *hybrida*) is a fall bloomer that shows up when just about everything else looks tired. The anemone cultivar 'Honorine Jobert', on the contrary, looks like a breath of fresh air—with delicate, springlike white petals around yellow centers, all nodding 3 to 4 feet above handsome, broad-leafed foliage in August and September. This is on the emeritus Plants of Merit listing for Missouri. A similar cultivar is the slightly shorter—at 2 to 3 feet— 'Queen Charlotte' with pink, semidouble blossoms. Yet another soft pink anemone  for shady fall gardens has a name that's a mouthful—*Anemone tomentosum* 'Robustis-sima'. Who doesn't need something robust at the end of a long, hot Missouri summer?

Peony is a favorite cut flower, its sweet, mild scent and old-fashioned look brightening up any room in those first few weeks of spring. In fact, Mother's Day and peonies are a wonderful yearly link. And when a peony's leaf is healthy and deep green, it makes for a great middle-of-the-border foliage plant after its flowers have been cut. Many Missouri gardeners favor the longtime hybrid *Paeonia* 'Krinkled White', with single flowers that start out pink and open to a bright, fresh white. The semidouble coral pink blooms of 'Coral Charm' and the semidouble yellow blooms with red centers of 'Garden Treasure' are other favorites. So are the reds in a ruffled peony 'Red Charm' as well as the fat, red blossoms of 'Many Happy Returns'. Go to www.peonies.net—the Web site of Bannister Garden Center in Raymore—for a great peony photo gallery plus order form. Also check out Hollingsworth Peonies of Maryville (www.hollingsworthpeonies.com). And the Heartland Peony Society (www.peonies.org) has peony events, plant sources, and other inside information for its members.

Phlox rules in some home gardens—in Ricki Creamer's near Kansas City, for instance. "There are so many new colors and mildew-resistant varieties," says Creamer, owner of Red Cedar Country Gardens there. "Have you seen the dwarf Flame series?" she asks. "They are great." She particularly likes *P. paniculata* 'Pink Flame' that grows a foot or so tall and produces large clusters of fragrant, tubular pink flowers with red eyes. Among her other favorites are the white 'David', a 2002 Perennial Plant of the Year (www.perennialplant.org); 'Laura', purple with a white eye; and 'Robert Poore', a violet pink and a Missouri Plant of Merit.

Rudbeckia conjures up images of yellow daisies with black centers—the classic black-eyed Susans. However, there are many rudbeckias. At Bowood Farms in St. Louis (www.bowoodfarms .com), for instance, there's *Rudbeckia fulgida* as part of an extensive native-plant selection, producing 2- to 3-foot-tall daisylike flowers June through October. These hardy plants tolerate drought as well as heat and humidity. A popular cultivar is 'Goldsturm', slightly more compact than its native parent. But take a look at the so-called sweet black-eyed Susans (*R. subtomentosa*)—"long-lived, taller, and better than regular black-eyed Susans," says a Bowood tag. One new cultivar of this latter *Rudbeckia* is 'Henry Eilers'—an intriguing twist with its golden yellow quilled petals around brown centers, all on airy 3- or 4-foot stems. Idyllwild Gardens in Savannah (www.idyllwildgardens.com) prizes it.

Salvia, or perennial ornamental sage, is important to butterfly gardeners, hummingbird lovers, and perennial growers alike. There are dozens of salvia types—witness a list on www .mobot.org/gardeninghelp/plantfinder. A favorite in Missouri is the relatively new *Salvia nemorosa* 'Caradonna'. It grows 1 to 2 feet tall and produces violet blue flowers on dark purple stems. It needs cutting back after flowering for continued upright growth. And it takes dry conditions well.

Sedum is another plant that takes dry conditions and blooms in late summer through fall. There are the 1- to 2-foot-tall sedums such as the old-timer *Sedum spectabile* 'Autumn Joy' and, more interestingly, the very small, ground-covering varieties of this plant, also called stonecrop. Jeff Oberhaus at Vintage Hill Farm in Franklin favors *S. rupestre* 'Angelina', at just about 6 inches tall with tiny yellow flowers June through August atop spiky, golden gray green leaves. It's perfect for the edge of a dry border. "They are all great for hot Kansas," agrees Ricki Creamer, of Red Cedar Country Gardens across the Missouri-Kansas line in the Kansas City area. "But I adore 'Angelina'," she says, "for its reddish orange winter color." Alternatively, in medium-wet and shady conditions, don't overlook the native *Sedum ternatum* if you have need for a low-growing, spring-flowering plant beside a pond or other water feature.

Roses, in Categories All of Their Own

A rose isn't a rose isn't a rose. It is a delicate hybrid tea, or a grandiflora, or a floribunda, or an elegant climber, or—nowadays—the array of disease-resistant, hardy shrubs that many perennial gardeners use as a way of returning to this flowering plant. Many of us don't like to spray with chemicals. And in Missouri's summer humidity, hybrid teas are among the fussy roses that require frequent chemical care. And so many gardens now look to shrub roses for their flowering perennial beds. Take *Rosa* 'Carefree Beauty', for instance. It is has abundant coral pink, fragrant roses from June to frost, on nicely shaped, 3- to 5-foot-tall deciduous shrubs with dark green foliage. A sister plant, 'Carefree Wonder', produces hot pink flowers. The late Griffith Buck of Iowa State University hybridized these and other black-spot- and mildew-resistant roses. In Missouri, Moffet Nursery and Garden Center of St. Joseph, not too far from the Iowa border, is one of the retailers specializing in the hardy Buck roses. Vintage Hill Farm in Franklin is another; visit www.vintagehill.com.

More recently, the trademarked Knock Out series of roses wowed perennial gardeners with consistent blooms and disease resistance. It is sold everywhere. The cherry red *R.* 'Radrazz' Knock Out is an outstanding performer, with a new sister shrub, the trademarked Double Knock Out, that has even fatter blooms and is as disease resistant but more compact and shade tolerant. These get rave reviews from home gardeners on the Missouri Botanical Garden's PlantFinder Web site (www.mobot.org/gardening help/plantfinder). "Outstanding in every way. Still blooming in November in my Zone 5 garden," writes one. And newest on the shrub-rose horizon is worth the long name—the trademarked Oso Easy Paprika, *R.* 'ChewMayTime,' mostly called Oso Easy. It's nearly a ground cover, producing sprays of reddish orange blossoms, each with single rows of petals, from midsummer to fall on shrubs that mound to 1 or 2 feet tall.

Stars of the climbing-rose scene, meanwhile, are the Canadian-developed 'William Baffin', with pink blooms and suberb winter hardiness; 'New Dawn', a blush pink that's also disease resistant; and 'Zephirine Drouhin', the one pink climber that's thornless and will take some shade. If you want to go the route of growing more delicate roses—or any roses, for that matter—go to the Web site of the American Rose Society (www.ars .org) and click on Contact Consulting Rosarians in Your Area. There are a dozen listed around the state of Missouri. Consulting rosarians are not unlike master gardeners—it is their volunteer responsibility to help other gardeners, in this case, with roses. Two other sites to consider for old-fashioned roses are www.heritage rosefoundation.org and www.heirloomroses.com.

Best Bulbs for Missouri

For spring color daffodils are by far the most reliable perennial bulbs for Missouri. Tulips are lovely, perhaps once. But during their second and third years, they cannot be counted on to come back. Missouri's dense, poorly drained clay soils and typically wet winters encourage tulip bulbs to decay. Let's face it: Tulips are native to Central Asia, where topsoil tends to be gravelly and extremely well draining. Even at the Missouri Botanical Garden, most of the thousand of tulips planted each year are treated as annuals and dug out after spring blooms. Most anything in the genus *Narcissus*, on the other hand, originated in damp mountain regions of Spain and Portugal. These daffodils and jonquils tend to thrive and multiply over the years in Missouri soils.

Here are just a few top perennial-bulb choices for spring blooms by Jason Delaney, a young bulb expert who's already a senior horticulturist at the Missouri Botanical Garden. He likes these daffodils: *Narcissus* 'Ice Follies', with white petals and open, sunny yellow cups, blooming early to midseason and growing to 18 inches tall; 'Tete-a-Tete', an early-blooming miniature daffodil—5 to 6 inches—with bright yellow petals and slightly darker yellow cups; 'Bravoure', a mid-spring bloomer with nearly perfect white petals and long, pale yellow cups; 'Carlton', a fragrant, heirloom daffodil with buttercup yellow blooms at 14 to 16 inches; and 'Glenfarclas', with trumpet-shaped, deep yellow flowers growing from 12 to 18 inches.

Besides daffodils for spring, Delaney favors such other perennial spring bloomers as *Hyacinthoides hispanica* 'Excelsior', or Spanish bluebell, a Plant of Merit heirloom bulb and vigorous producer of deep blue to lavender bell-shaped flowers on 10- to 12-inch stems; *Leucojum aestivum* 'Gravetye Giant', or summer snowflake, looking like a giant lily-of-the-valley with small, nodding white blooms on 18- to 24-inch stems; *Chionodoxa sardensis*, or glory-of-the-snow, a 4- to 6-inch blue heirloom that blooms early, a perfect companion to Narcissus 'Tete-a-Tete'; and *Camassia leichtlinii*

'Caerulea', a 2- to 3-foot, blue to lavender bloomer for the middle or back of a late-spring border.

A few of Delaney's summer–fall bulb choices are *Lilium* 'Scheherazade', an Orienpet lily with 10-foot-tall stems bearing white-edged red blooms, from a relatively new group of spectacular, heat-tolerant crosses of fragrant Oriental lilies with large-flowered trumpet lilies; *Crinum bulbispermum*, or orange river lily, which blooms from May through June with white and pink petals striped in red and has the best winter hardiness of the crinums in Zone 6; *Lycoris chinensis*, golden surprise lily or spider lily, with variable yellow or golden coloration; *Colchicum speciosum*, autumn crocus, with lavender pink fall blooms that are surprisingly like spring crocus; and *Allium stellatum*, prairie onion, a 1- to 2-foot-tall Missouri native with rounded reddish pink blooms from July to September.

CHAPTER EIGHT

Trees and Shrubs

"Have you seen our trees?" asked a somber Springfield horticulturist. Indeed I had, on a recent May visit there. Still horrendous were the side effects of an ice storm the previous January that had left thousands of mature trees, months later, ragged, broken, and leafless above a spring-green layer below. "I have experienced some bad ice storms," said Pat Scammahorn, of Wickman's Garden Village in this Ozarks city—the third largest in the state. "But this was the worst ice storm I've ever seen in my life." By August new shade trees and flowering ones were best sellers of Wickman's summer season.

Springfield's experience is just one example of how important trees are—or are coming to be—to Missourians. This is, after all, a state with a tree's bloom—the snowy white blossom of the native downy hawthorn (*Crataegus mollis*)—as the official state flower. And the equally lovely flowering dogwood (*Cornus florida*) is Missouri's official tree. However, trees weren't always revered in the state. By 1920, according to the Missouri Department of Conservation, the state's great stands of oak, hickory, pine, and red cedar had been logged by businessmen from the East so that "the forests that no one thought would run out, did." It was not until 1929 that a forest association successfully lobbied the state legislature to permit purchase of land for national forests. Conservation efforts on the state level also grew. Today fourteen million acres, or 31 percent of Missouri, is in forest cover, according to the conservation department. That compares with an estimated 70 percent of the state when early explorers made their way west. There is room for more trees.

The Function of Trees and Shrubs in the Landscape

Why grow trees and shrubs? They are beautiful features of lawn or garden, giving height and punctuation to a space. Witness, for instance, the wide-open branches and tall, stately trunk of the Missouri native black gum (*Nyssa sylvatica*). This tree seems poised to embrace. And it's as good a specimen as you're likely find for a roomy yard or garden that also has good water supplies. It has a history of being hard to transplant, but at least one Missouri grower is making a difference there (see the "Native Son" sidebar in this chapter). Otherwise, black gum is very low maintenance; likes moist, even poorly draining soil; has dark green leaves in summer that turn yellow, orange, red, and purple in fall; and draws bees to nectar from its late-spring flowers and birds for the resulting fruits in fall.

But besides providing beauty, this tree—like many others that do well in the state—helps control climate with shade, absorbs pollutants from the air, and produces oxygen in return. According to a recently launched United Nations Environment Program, with a goal of planting one billion trees around the world, "Planting trees remains the cheapest, most effective means of drawing excess carbon dioxide from the atmosphere." And shrubs—many of them, basically, smaller trees—do the same work on pollution while helping to shade houses at the foundations and, in turn, helping to reduce heating and cooling costs. But shrubs also are coming to serve another purpose, according to several Missouri garden designers: They're taking the place of certain flowering perennials that may require too much care for too little payback. Shrubs, particularly ones with winter interest, look good in the perennial bed year-round.

Siting a New Tree

Severe storms in Missouri in recent years have sent horticulturists and arborists scrambling, not only to help homeowners prune out damage but also to aid in choosing good, safe trees as replacements. One of the most important considerations these days is where to site new trees. If electrical lines are nearby, says Roger Branson of Droege Tree Care Company in St. Louis, "generally you want something that's not going to get tall." He recommends dogwoods and eastern redbuds near lines where there's also part shade, and some of the newer crab apples—resistant to common diseases—for full sun. So does Kansas City Power & Light, which gives out free, printed brochures called *Right Tree in the Right Place;* an online version is available at www.kcpl.com. Such information from St. Louis' Ameren utility is at www.ameren.com/ environment.

"Planting tall-growing trees under and near lines," says the International Society of Arboriculture (ISA) on one of its two Web sites, www.treesaregood.com, "eventually requires your utility to prune them to maintain safe clearance from the wires. This pruning may result in the tree having an unnatural appearance. Periodic pruning can also lead to a shortened life span for the tree. Trees that must be pruned away from power lines are under greater stress and are more susceptible to insects and disease."

You can't plant what will become a big specimen too close to the house either. After some summer and winter storms tore down electrical lines in the St. Louis area, homeowners seemed extra wary of that. "I didn't see that much of the surge to refor-est," says Bill Spradley, of the Kirkwood company Trees, Forests & Landscapes. "There's been some replanting but not aggressive replanting. I'm kind of surprised. In some areas I'd guess they lost as much as 30 percent of the canopy. But I think right now, there's a little fear of putting trees near the house."

So what to site near a structure? Not trees in the 30- to 50-foot range, such as black gums, which also need 20 to 30 feet to spread out at maturity. "Plant large trees at least 35 feet away from the house for proper root development and to minimize damage to the house or building," says the ISA, the arboriculture group. "These large-growing trees are also recommended for streets without overhead restrictions." Twenty feet is the closest you should go with a medium to small tree, unless it is a true dwarf, such as certain Japanese maples.

Pruning an Existing Tree

Springfield's Cindy Garner is urban forester for the southwest region of Missouri. And she fields questions daily about pruning injured, old, or storm-damaged trees. Homeowners are amazed, she says, at how resilient their trees are and that they see new growth a week or so after damage by ice or wind. But she cautions them to wait and watch the trees before doing any major pruning and then to make sure they choose a good professional or make the right cuts themselves. For a good tree trimmer, she suggests going to a second Web site of the International Society of Arboriculture—go to www.isa-arbor.com, click on the home page, then on Verify a Certification to get to a page where you can plug in your postal code (zip code in this country) to find dozens of folks who are certified to do good work.

Otherwise, if you do it yourself, she has further advice: "We use what we call a three-step method," she says, referring to guidelines in a simple, two-page handout titled *Basic Pruning Guidelines* published by the Missouri Department of Conservation and available at www.mdc.mo.gov. That guide was extremely popular after one recent storm, Garner says. Among other techniques, the guide advises: "Branches 1 inch in diameter or larger should generally be removed in a series of three cuts." Several sketches show how—and how not—to cut. "This will prevent bark attached to the base of the cut branch from stripping away bark on the trunk as it falls." Ideas for preventive maintenance and pruning on healthy trees also may be found in the guide.

Best Trees for Missouri

What not to plant is as important a question these days as asking: Which trees are good for Missouri yards? Ash trees, unfortunately, are not advised now, in the wake of the emerald ash borer bearing down on several states. Sidewalks on spacious grounds around the famous Gateway Arch in St. Louis, for instance, are lined with 'Rosehill' white ash (*Fraxinus americana*). According to David Bubac, chief of facilities management at the Arch's Jefferson National Expansion Memorial, "We're down about four hundred trees due to storms. We also have maples and bald cypress along the Mississippi Riverfront. But the cultural landscape report requires us to replace ash with ash. We're monitoring the trees and have good contacts with several universities. I sent our gardening supervisor up to a session on emerald ash borer. At this point, we're studying the situation." Some other trees on a number of not-to-plant lists include the American elm and Siberian elm (Dutch elm disease) and Bradford pear (weak branch structure, although the 'Cleveland' selections of this street tree are a bit of an improvement). And in the category of trees with messy fruits, branches, or nuts, there is the mulberry, pin oak, sweet gum, and walnut. It's a personal choice.

Here's what works:

American linden (*Tilia americana*) is an addition to the Missouri Plants of Merit list for 2009, specifically the cultivar 'Redmond'. It grows 50 to 70 feet tall in full sun to part shade and is easily grown in medium-moist soils, although it will tolerate some drought. It's not so keen on dense urban settings, but in late spring it produces fragrant pale yellow flowers and large, dark green leaves.

American smoke tree (*Cotinus obovatus*) is a 2008 Plant of Merit and a small, rounded, Missouri native, growing to between 20 and 30 feet tall. Its blue green leaves turn spectacular colors of yellow, orange, red, and purple in fall. When flower clusters are spent, the remaining hairy structures take on the ethereal quality of purplish pink "smoke."

Dogwoods, including the white-flowering Missouri state tree (*Cornus florida*), are lovely, lacy harbingers of spring, with pink or white bracts floating out from 20-foot-tall trunks. Because the fungal disease spot anthracnose has devastated dogwoods in the Northeast, disease-resistant varieties are the only way to go in Missouri. 'Appalachian Spring' is one—a new, white-bracted variety of *C. florida* with large, prolific blooms, a lovely upright shape, and anthracnose resistance. Other cultivars less susceptible to the disease include 'Cherokee Princess' and 'Cherokee Brave' as well as the hardy crosses with Chinese dogwood (*C. kousa*)—check out 'Satomi', with faded pink blooms. And don't overlook Cornelian cherry dogwood (*C. mas*), a lovely flowering short tree or tall shrub that's good for smaller landscapes. It is a Plant of Merit emeritus.

Ginkgo (*Ginkgo biloba*) is one of the best medium-size trees for full sun in Missouri and a 2008 choice for Plant of Merit. Visit the Missouri Botanical Garden and you'll see a healthy, one-hundred-year-plus male ginkgo near the geodesic dome called the Climatron. These disease-free natives of China may grow to between 50 and 80 feet tall and adapt well to many conditions, including road salt, heat, and pollution. Cultivars called 'Autumn Gold' and 'Princeton Century' are especially desirable. Plant only ginkgo males; females produce messy fruit with a foul odor.

Magnolia. For starters, sweet bay magnolia (*Magnolia virginiana* var. *australis*) is a long-standing Plant of Merit and a native to the southeastern United States. In Zone 5 it appreciates a protected location and will tolerate shade but prefers full sun. It produces lemon-scented, white flowers in midspring that continue sporadically throughout the summer. The shiny green foliage is evergreen in the South and semievergreen to deciduous in much of Missouri. However, the trademarked *Magnolia* Moonglow 'Jim Wilson' is a selection by Earl Cully of Illinois—just north of St. Louis—that has more of an evergreen tendency for the region. And if you want to try a true southern magnolia, the Plants of Merit program says to go for *M. grandiflora* 'Bracken's Brown Beauty'—"a significant cultivar because, unlike the species, it is reliably winter hardy to the St. Louis area," says the Missouri Botanical Garden's PlantFinder service. Indeed, on the University of Missouri campus in the center of the state, a Bracken's magnolia grows well on the north side of several campus buildings. For more information on magnolias, go to www.magnoliasociety.org.

Maples. Look at English hedge maple (*Acer campestre*) for a European solution to elegant screening. "It drapes all the way to the ground," says Kirkwood arborist Bill Spradley, "and is very hardy here." It can be pruned to form a tall hedge. It's an addition to the Plants of Merit list for 2009. Building a collection of Japanese maples (*A. palmatum*), on the other hand, may be limited only by an ability to afford new specimens and by decisions on dissected (cut) leaves versus palmate (palm shaped) ones. However, any of these generally dwarf, mounded, deciduous trees with bright fall color should be sited in locations protected from wind and as much as possible from late-spring frosts. If given some afternoon shade, the leaves should not scorch in full-on Missouri summer sun. Red maples (*A. rubrum*), on the other hand, are tough, tall—40 to 60 feet—Missouri natives that hybridizers have used to develop such excellent cultivars as 'October Glory' and 'Red Sunset', the latter called "one of the best red maple cultivars available in commerce," says the PlantFinder service of the Missouri Botanical Garden. Meanwhile, a new trademarked *A. rubrum* Burgundy Belle is becoming a favorite in the landscaping business. It was selected from a northeast Kansas location and has thick leaves that make it a good choice for harsher climates.

Norway spruce (*Picea abies*). 'Acrocona' is a cultivar of the generally 40- to 60-foot-tall pyramidal evergreen conifer, called "our toughest evergreen" by Kirkwood arborist Bill Spradley. 'Acrocona' is compact—used as a shrub in some circumstances— growing only to about 5 to 10 feet at maturity. It has dark green needles and is noted for producing showy red cones at the branch ends in spring. It is an addition to the 2008 list of Missouri Plants of Merit.

Oaks. The trees of the genus *Quercus* haven't been widely used in modern landscapes because they're fairly hard to transplant. But they are strong, tough Missouri natives. And with new techniques (see the "Native Son" sidebar), these hardy trees— especially swamp white oak (*Q. bicolor*) and bur oak (*Q. macrocarpa*)—are good choices for home gardeners with yards big

Native Son

Wayne Lovelace, of Forrest Keeling Nursery in Elsberry, is a man with a mission to make native trees easier to transplant. They have "very dominant taproots," he says, that are tough to move from one place to another, and in the tree business, that's not helpful. So Lovelace has invented a new technique for starting the natives from seed in a "bottomless flat in the greenhouse," he says, "where the air circulates under a bench. When each taproot hits the air, the tip dries and dies and induces a large formation of lateral root systems rather than a long taproot." The process—including additional steps—now is patented. And just in time for two surges of activity: One is that the fifty-year-plus Forrest Keeling operation has opened a retail business to complement its longtime whole-sale venture. See them at www.fknursery.com. Another is a return to "the environmental movement," as Lovelace puts it, "and now a lot of businesses are thinking that green is the way to go. But it makes sense when you consider all the merits of natives," he says. "They don't require any fertilizer once they're established, they can overcome any of the diseases, insect problems, and the weather extremes, including cold and drought."

enough for a broad spread of branches as much as 50 to 60 feet wide. Swamp white oak likes moist to wet soils, as the name implies, so it's a good choice for low spots and other wet ground. The new trademarked *Q. bicolor* Regal Prince is more of an upright, vigorous grower that's tolerant of both wet and dry soils and is a good choice for smaller yards. Bur oak is a beautiful oak that may grow to a height of between 60 to 80 feet with plentiful acorns—each with a bur near the rim—that mature in a single year and provide food for wildlife. Look for more new cultivars coming out for Missouri.

Redbud (*Cercis canadensis*), the Missouri native, is small at around 20 feet tall and delightful in spring, when tiny purple pink flowers bloom profusely on bare branches. There are so many good varieties now to consider. But the cultivar 'Royal White' is a bud of a different color. It is "uncommonly found in commerce," says PlantFinder, on the Missouri Botanical Garden Web site. But it's worth asking for at your favorite garden center. That's why 'Royal White' is added to the 2008 Plants of Merit list for Missouri. And for a small graceful specimen tree, consider the new weeping Lavender Twist redbud discovered in the early 1990s in New York State in Connie Covey's garden. 'Covey' is the cultivar name and Lavender Twist is the trademark name for a tree reaching 6 to 10 feet tall at maturity.

River birch. The trademarked Heritage river birch 'Cully' (*Betula nigra*) is a now popular, fast-growing cultivar with cream-colored exfoliating bark and leathery dark green leaves that are larger and glossier than those of the species. Earl Cully, the Illinois hybridizer, found the original plant growing in a St. Louis yard and got the owner's permission to propagate it for his business, Heritage Trees, Inc. It's now on the emeritus list of Plants of Merit. Another new river birch introduction has the ungainly trademarked name of 'BNMTF' Dura-Heat but is said, on the PlantFinder Web site, to have "better tolerance to summer heat, better insect and disease resistance, and superior foliage to the species."

Tulip tree (*Liriodendron tulipifera*). No siting near electrical wires for this specimen—one of the tallest hardwood trees in east-

More on Trees

- Tree-planting tips from the Arbor Day Foundation's Web site (www.arborday.org/trees/ninethings.cfm) comes in the form of a neat list of "Nine Things You Should Know about Trees," including excellent, if abbreviated, planting guides for both containerized and bare-root trees.

- Nearly free trees. The Missouri Forestry Division operates the George O. White State Forest Nursery at Licking. You can purchase tree and shrub seedlings at minimal cost for conservation plantings on private lands. Obtain order forms online at http://mdc.mo.gov/forest/nursery/seedling or at your local Department of Conservation office, MU Extension center, or Soil and Water Conservation District office. You can order from November through mid-February on a first-come, first-served basis.

- An e-mailed tree-news quarterly, called *Green Horizons*, from MU Extension. Join up by going to http://extension.missouri.edu/explore/subscribe.

- Tree diseases in Missouri are discussed by staffers at the University of Missouri Extension Plant Diagnostic Clinic at http://soilplantlab.missouri.edu/plant/diseases/index.htm.

ern North America, reportedly reaching 90 to 150 feet in height at maturity. It has a strong straight trunk and broad conical habit and produces yellow and orange, tuliplike, cup-shaped flowers in spring. And it does well all over the state. As arborist Bill Spradley puts it, "If tulip poplars begin to bloom in the Bootheel region around May 15, in Columbia they should bloom five days later, and in Lancaster on the Iowa border, they should bloom ten days later."

Best Shrubs for Missouri

Steffie Littlefield is all about shrubs. This hardworking horticulturist and garden designer at Garden Heights Nursery (www.gardenheights.com) in Richmond Heights is advising home gardeners to use shrubs more, even more than flowering perennials in some cases, for easy care in spring, summer, and fall plus structure in winter. In her yard? "It's fifty-fifty," she says, half shrubs, such as crape myrtle, hardy hydrangea, and hibiscus—all inherited from the garden of her late grandmother, who'd been an active volunteer for garden clubs as well as the Missouri Botanical Garden. Littlefield has added her own, newer dwarf varieties as well as such staples for winter interest as redtwig and yellowtwig dogwood. She's also mixed in a number of disease-resistant shrub roses. And she really values the screening and "layering effect" that she gets from evergreens—all planted alongside the flowers. Here are more ideas on shrubs from Littlefield and others.

Azaleas. "Pay a little more for the hardiest varieties," says Linda Banta, plant-sales chairman for the Charleston garden club that hosts a charming Dogwood-Azalea Festival on the third weekend of April each year. "Dogwoods were known in the area forever," she says of this southeastern Missouri community, located at the top of the Bootheel. Indeed, dogwoods grow wild in dappled shade and on acidic, rocky soils alongside some of Missouri's native azaleas and rhododendrons. But cultivated azaleas became the hobby of a Charleston dentist's wife in the 1950s. She started a club in honor of her gardening neighbor, Molly French. The Molly French Garden Club celebrated its fortieth year of festivals in 2008. A favorite shade-loving azalea variety for this southeastern region of Missouri town is *Rhododendron* 'Delaware Valley White'—a spreading evergreen azalea with spectacular midseason blooms of white flowers that are 2½ inches wide. 'Delaware Valley White' is not reliably winter hardy throughout Zone 5, although it's wintered well in St. Louis in most recent years. Look at www.mobot.org/gardeninghelp/plantfinder for even tougher azaleas, good through winters in Zones 3 and 4; see more about the festival and plant sale at www.charlestonmo.org/festival.asp; and go to www.azaleas.org—the Azalea Society of America—for excellent cultural information on the shrubs.

Beautyberry (*Callicarpa dichotoma*) is another "southern-style" shrub—this one a deciduous Asian native sporting incredibly bright purple berries in fall. It does best in areas such as Springfield in southwest Missouri, a solid Zone 6. But farther north, in Zone 5, it also overwinters if planted in protected spots. The Missouri Botanical Garden advises to prune "stems back to 6 inches in late winter each year" since beautyberry flowers on new wood. The cultivar 'Early Amethyst' is a Plant of Merit for 2008.

Boxwood has a huge following in more formal gardens in many parts of the state, even though late spring freezes may brown up unprotected plants. But the boxwood *Buxus sinica* var. *insularis* 'Wintergreen' is, as its name suggests, hardier and less likely to go bronze in winter. Its compactness—at a maximum of 4 feet tall and 5 feet wide at maturity—makes it a good low hedge as well as a good fit as a perennial-border specimen.

Buttonbush (*Cephalanthus occidentalis*) is native to just about every Missouri county. And yet it is ornamental enough to make it onto the must-have lists of many horticulturists. "The buttonbush is best planted in wet locations," says Dianne O'Connell, owner of the St. Louis–area garden-design company Landscapes

Alive, "but it can be a real asset in many landscapes." Its rounded white flowers in June and July "are also welcome at that time of the year," she says. The Plants of Merit listers agree, adding buttonbush in 2008.

Clethra, or sweet pepperbush (*Clethra alnifolia*), is a medium-size, trouble-free shrub for wet soils and full sun to part shade. Beyond that it produces fragrant, white bottlebrush-type blooms in July and August. Cluster it with other shrubs that like regularly watered conditions, such as inkberry and redtwig dogwood.

Crape myrtle (*Lagerstroemia indica*) may grow to 20 feet in Steffie Littlefield's St. Louis–area backyard—it is her grandmother's plant and one that's been cut back many times after frost. But Littlefield also is fond of the new, more compact forms, such as the lavender 'Zuni' and the white 'Hopi'—with good mildew resistance and winter damage only occasionally to top growth. Just keep in mind that some crape myrtles in the St. Louis area "were at such a vulnerable stage of growth" before a recent, unprecedented late-spring freeze, says Missouri Botanical Garden horticulturist Chip Tynan, "that many were killed to the ground when their sap froze and expanded, damaging vital cambium tissue. If people want crape myrtles," he adds, "the best way to grow them may be as a cut-back shrub or a garden perennial." Also look at the new trademarked crape myrtle Rosey Carpet in Chris Schaul's display beds at Wine Country Gardens in Defiance. It is a spreading, foot-tall pink ground cover, of all things, massed there along with the equally tiny, new mounding rose called Oso Easy Paprika.

Forsythia, as in the trademarked *Forsythia* 'Courtasol' Gold Tide, is a dwarf—at 2 feet tall, 4 feet wide—of this wonderful, old-fashioned harbinger of spring. Use it in borders, along foundations, or mass planted on sunny slopes. Oval, medium green leaves stay attractive through fall. The Plants of Merit selection committee has put it on its emeritus list.

Hydrangeas "have had somewhat of a revival over the last few years," says Jennifer Schamber, horticulturist at Greenscape Gardens in Ballwin, "most likely due to the introduction of the Endless Summer," she says of the big-leafed, pink-blooming *Hydrangea macrophylla* 'Bailmer' Endless Summer. 'Blushing Bride' Endless Summer is a new sister plant. But other forms of hydrangeas have been the ones to make it onto the Plants of Merit honor roll. Oakleaf hydrangea (*H. quercifolia*) is on the list as "a handsome and native American shrub." *H. arborescens*, the midsize Missouri native with dainty white blossoms, is there, too. A cultivar of *H. arborescens*, by the way, may be an all-time favorite in some Missouri yards—the shade shrub with snowball-like flowers called 'Annabelle'. And climbing hydrangea (*H. anomala* subspecies *petiolaris*) is not to be missed, for it offers deep green heart-shaped leaves, fragrant white flowers, and exfoliating bark with year-round interest.

Itea, or sweetspire (*Itea virginica*), 'Henry's Garnet' is yet another Plant of Merit and a fragrant, rounded cultivar—maturing to about 3 feet tall—with cylindrical clusters of tiny white flowers in May and June, dark green leaves that redden in fall, and burgundy stems in winter.

Lilac (*Syringa reticulata*) is a Japanese import, a large shrub or small tree with an old-fashioned, easily recognized fragrance and a need to grow in full sun. The

In drought, trees and shrubs need watering, just as does any other plant. Newly planted trees and shrubs need it even more. But the Missouri Department of Conservation (http://mdc.mo.gov/forest) goes beyond the advice of a single application of water equal to 1 or 2 inches of rainfall a week. It says that to test for soil dryness, dig a hole about 6 to 8 inches deep at the edge of the root zone and perform a squeeze test. That is, "squeeze a lump of soil from the bottom of the hole and roll it between two fingers. If soil feels sticky or gummy, soil is wet. If soil sticks together and forms a ball or ribbon, soil moisture is probably adequate for established trees. If soil crumbles apart or powders, soil is dry, and trees would benefit from more watering. Heavy, clay soils absorb water more slowly than sandy or gravelly soils, but can take in more water and hold it longer."

brand-new cultivar 'Snow Dance', by the large grower Bailey Nurseries, is said to be more treelike, with a vase-shaped habit, very dark green foliage, and a heavy set of creamy white flowers. But a dwarf has captured Steffie Littlefield's attention. The compact *S. meyeri* 'Dream Dwarf Lilac' features "little leaves that have a nice little wavy edge to them," says Littlefield. "People love that texture. It also seems to be very powdery-mildew resistant."

Redtwig dogwood (*Cornus sericea* 'Cardinal') is multistemmed, rapidly growing—to a maximum of 6 feet—and spectacular as bare, red upright stems in winter. Its highly colorful, dogwood-shrub cousins include yellowtwig (*C. sericea* 'Flaviramea') and bloodtwig (*C. sanguinea*).

Lawns

Like eighty-five million households in this country that "take part in lawn and garden activities," according to the National Gardening Association, Missouri homeowners love their turf and flowers. But especially their turf. In fact, there are more folks in the state who care for lawn than garden. "I would say that 75 to 80 percent of Missouri households still mow their own lawns," says Brad S. Fresenburg, extension research associate at the University of Missouri Turfgrass Research Center. The rest hire that work out. "I feel most homeowners find it easier to maintain the lawn than do landscaping and flower beds," he adds. "For most, it's not that they don't want such things around their home. It's a time and knowledge issue." Bruce Butterfield, research director for the National Gardening Association, tends to agree. Thirty-three percent of U.S. households in a recent survey for his group "have a flower garden," he says. "In point of fact, more people do lawn care nationwide than do flower gardening."

What are the functions of lawns in the landscape? Lawn is not just a covering of bare soil. The English helped invent the closely cut lawn for walks and games. Noblemen and women came to like the status that pristine turf gave their estates. A perfect lawn sent the message that they could afford servants to keep the grass scythed and, later, cut with the English invention of the push mower circa 1830. Modern American lawns, says Paul Roberts, a turf expert and coordinator of the horticulture program at St. Louis Community College's Meramec campus, "serve several functions to the homeowner. They do prevent erosion," he says. "But after the invention of the gasoline engine, the homeowner thinks of lawn as the ornamental accessory to the home, and they do everything they can to make it the best—and the competition is on. It's always the status issue as to who has the healthiest lawn, who has the greenest lawn, even who has best mowing pattern. For the same reason that people buy the coolest cars and want the best architecture on their homes, people like to have a nice environment."

What Is Turfgrass?

When you talk "turf," you go beyond lawn and into the worlds of golf courses, sports fields, racecourses, and other pristine installations. Turf, in these arenas, is a low grass on which to stroll, run, even race horses. But the term "turf-type" has evolved in this country to help distinguish newer, better cultivars, principally turf-type tall fescues (*Festuca* species) that are vast improvements over the tall fescues introduced here in the early nineteenth century and that have become invasive in pastures and along roadsides around Missouri. But then, all commercial grasses for lawn—with the exception of native buffalo grass—were brought here from Europe and Asia. All exotics have the potential of escaping into the wild. (See chapter 10 for a discussion of invasive exotics.)

Roberts is one of a number of experts around the country who aid in the process of collecting data on new cultivars of turf. His acre-size space on the Meramec campus is part of the National Turfgrass Evaluation Program. Go to www.ntep.org if you want to see statistical tables on some recent tests from similar plots on the University of Missouri's Columbia campus—managed by Brad Fresenburg—as well as from Meramec's campus near St. Louis. "I've been evaluating literally hundreds of varieties of bluegrass, fescue, Bermuda grass, and ryegrass," Roberts says. "The official NTEP tests sites are done at colleges and universities to assure that there's little bias in the ratings of these things, so it helps to get the best products to the homeowners. And it also helps the companies to market different products to different regions of the country."

What's the Best Turf for Missouri?

Roberts and his fellow testers get this question all the time. There's not one easy answer for much of the state. He explains it this way. The mid regions of the country are girdled by a belt called the "transition zone." Think of a line that moves west from Virginia and North Carolina, through West Virginia, Kentucky, parts of southern Ohio, Indiana, and Illinois, through St. Louis and east across Missouri into Kansas. It is the transition between northern and southern regions for turfgrass. Neither so-called warm-season nor cool-season grasses are completely comfortable here. On the northern edge of the transition zone in Missouri is Kirksville—30 miles or so from the Iowa border—where cool-season grasses, such as Kentucky bluegrass, perennial ryegrass, and turf-type tall fescue thrive when temperatures are at around 60 to 75 degrees. On the transition zone's south side is the state's border with Arkansas and Tennessee. All of central Missouri is in transition, and much of the southern part of the state teeters between cool- and warm-season grasses—the latter growing optimally in temperatures of 80 to 95 degrees. Zoysia, Bermuda grass, even buffalo grass do best in such heat.

Ask Paul Roberts what to plant, especially in the populous areas of Kansas City, Columbia, Jefferson City, and St. Louis. "There really is not any one thing that's the best" in the transition zone, Roberts replies. "I tell people here to plant what you like. If you really love that thick carpet of zoysia, be happy with that. Zoysia is relatively easy to manage," he says, of the low-growing, heat-loving, drought-tolerant grass that is slow to establish but eventually takes over a space and aggressively competes with weeds. It is lush and green for six warm months of the year, but

Turf Tips Online

Zoysia-growing tips may be found in Brad Fresenburg's excellent *Establishment and Care of Zoysiagrass Lawns,* MU Extension Guide G6706, found at http://extension.missouri.edu/explore. Check out other guides, such as *Cool Season Grasses: Lawn Establishment and Renovation* (G6700); *Cool Season Grasses: Lawn Maintenance Calendar* (G6705); *Home Lawn Watering Guide* (G6720); *Grasses in Shade: Establishing and Maintaining Lawns in Low Light* (G6725); and *Turfgrass Disease Control* (G6756).

Fresenburg's collection of online MEG newsletters for Missouri Environment and Garden are even more detailed in that they list top turf cultivars by name and sources for these cultivars in Missouri. For instance, check out his MEG newsletter titled *Selecting Turfgrasses for Missouri* by first going to the MEG Web site under the university's Plant Protection Programs—http://ppp.missouri.edu/newsletters/meg—and typing in the newsletter's title.

dormant—even wheat colored—in the transition zone in winter. "The important thing with growing zoysia," he says, "is not to apply a lot of nitrogen to it. If it grows fast, it tends to build up a lot of thatch on top of the soil, and the plant has a hard time growing through that."

If you like a fine-leafed, deep green carpet of cool-season bluegrass, you're not alone in Missouri. "There are lots of straight bluegrass lawns out there," even in the transition zone, says Roberts. In the St. Louis area, for instance, bluegrass will "green up basically in March and maintain a pretty good healthy lawn until about June," he says, "when it may start browning up in the heat. In summer here, bluegrass also is prone to a number of diseases and insects. In September it greens back up again." Bluegrass roots tend to be shallow, "6 inches, if you're lucky," says

Roberts, and so drought affects it more than, say, the cool-season grass that is a deeper-rooted turf-type tall fescue.

That brings us back to the turf-type fescues. An early, coarser fescue called K-31—"K" for Kentucky, where it was discovered in the 1930s—has been used widely in central and northern Missouri for years, growing best when it's cool but going dormant during hot, dry weather. K-31 is easy to find and not too expensive. And yet it has coarse leaves and a tendency to clump in dry conditions, although it is somewhat drought resistant. Newest varieties of turf-type tall fescue, however, have become very popular Missouri grasses. In good soil their roots may go down as deep as 2 feet and can make these grasses very drought tolerant indeed. Aesthetically, fescue's broader blades may never be able to compete with the fineness of bluegrass. And tall fescue, says Roberts, "is a little bit more prone to brown patch disease," a fungal disease that shows up as small circular patches of brown grass that may enlarge and join together. Overfertilizing and overwatering may contribute to this problem;

increasing sunlight and air circulation—even with a light pruning of nearby trees and shrubs—and reducing water and fertilizer may clear it up before resorting to fungicide.

Even better is to install a blend of fescues, so that if one is diseased or fails in some way, others fill in. "Several varieties of turf-type tall fescue offer superior resistance to brown patch and therefore will improve turf quality," Fresenburg says. "The number of seed products being sold over the counter can be overwhelming to homeowners." And so, on the extension and other MU Web sites, he lists a number of, but by no means all, top turf-type tall fescue blends by name to help consumers with the tough job of selecting seed.

This list of brand-name blends includes Revolution (sold in Missouri at many Westlake Ace Hardware stores); Winning Colors, under the Greenview label at retailers (Ace Hardware, or through the Web site, www.greenviewfertilizer.com); All-Pro (from MFA, Missouri Farmers Association); Pennington Tall Fescue Blend (Lowe's); Rebel Supreme Blend (also Lowe's); Rebel Elite (Home Depot); and Scott's Classic Tall Fescue Blend (Lowe's and Home Depot).

Fresenburg goes a step further to single out as most effective the blends of 90 percent turf-type tall fescues with 10 percent bluegrass. "Of all mixtures," he adds, the 90/10 fescue/bluegrass combination "is possibly the best for Missouri." And some brand names in this category, he says, include Revolution Plus (by special order, Westlake Ace Hardware stores), Tournament Quality Ultra Premium Fescue Plus Lawn Mixture (Lowe's), Pennington Tall Fescue and Kentucky Blue Grass Lawn Seed Mixture (Lowe's), and Master Turf Ultimate Blue Lawn Seed Mixture (Wal-Mart).

When asked what seed's responsible for his own pristine, green lawn, Paul Roberts volunteers that it's the all-turf-type-tall-fescue mix called Winning Colors—an early blend of four fescues without bluegrass. He wishes that a 90/10 mix had been available when he seeded. "The theory behind putting a little bit of bluegrass in there," Roberts says, "is that it spreads by rhizomes, so that when the fescue fades, you pretty much have an even lawn. And the varieties of tall fescues they're using now have narrower leaves. It's funny how they've taken fescue and made it look like bluegrass."

A word of warning to consumers from Fresenburg: "Any grass seed mixture with perennial ryegrass should not exceed 20 percent perennial rye, as it is susceptible to disease. Ryegrass is not very heat or drought tolerant. . . . Many of these seed products are packaged for national sales," he says, "and while they are excellent products for many areas of the country, they are not the best for the type of climate we deal with in Missouri. Concentrate more on the products that are tall fescue and Kentucky bluegrass blends, or mixtures of tall fescue and Kentucky bluegrass. By doing this, the selection becomes more narrow and simplified."

Buffalo grass (*Buchloe dactyloides*) is a warm-season native that seems to be growing on home gardeners. Or at least they're showing curiosity about this relatively short turf. Traces of it have been found in fossils in Kansas that date back at least seven million years. Buffalo grass was forage for the American bison, hence the name. And it is well adapted to dry conditions, such as in and around former prairie lands of Kansas City. But healthy patches of buffalo grass also show up elsewhere in the state: as portions of lawn at the EarthWays Center of the Missouri Botanical Garden in St. Louis; at the Whitmire Wildflower Garden of Shaw Nature Reserve in Gray Summit; and on the Island Garden surrounded by a large lake at Powell Gardens near Kansas City.

"It is a neat grass," says Roberts, whose Meramec campus also has a slightly sloped curbside patch edging a parking lot. "It's tough. You can plant it in areas that you don't want to maintain." His gets mowed once or twice a year. "It's very drought and also flood tolerant, but it doesn't necessarily set up to be a nice, dense grass that people would want for a lawn. It's a very loose and open grass." However, sources such as Missouri Wildflowers Nursery in Jefferson City are selling buffalo grass for "a lot of lawns in the Midwest," according to the nursery's growing guide found online at www.mo wildflowers.net. It sells seeds for a 'Cody' cultivar of buffalo grass, one "designed for lawns" that also does well "in compact clay soil and sun." 'Sharp's Improved' is another "reportedly vigorous variety" that's established by seed, sod, or plugs, says the online PlantFinder service of the Missouri Botanical Garden. And for installation of such a lawn, see the MU Guide G6730, *Establishment and Care of Buffalograss Lawns,* at http://extension .missouri.edu/explore/agguides/hort.

Trends in Lawn Care

The top new trend, says Bruce Butterfield of the National Gardening Association, is organic, or natural, lawn care. This is not to say that hundreds of thousands of home gardeners are heading out to purchase compost and fish emulsion to spread on their lawns. In a survey cosponsored by *Organic Gardening* magazine, Butterfield found that "while only 5 percent of U.S. households now use only all-natural fertilizer, insect, and weed control, some 21 percent said they would definitely or probably do so in the future. It says to me," according to Butterfield, "that it's going mainstream."

"It just makes sense to me to use organic materials," agrees Roberts, singling out the slow-release nature of organic fertilizer products. "You don't get the surge of nitrogen with slow release, and that's the biggest issue with maintaining turf. Water-soluable fertilizers leach into the soil too quickly, and grass is not able to absorb it all. I've seen research that shows a loss of 68 percent of nitrogen through leaching, so the grass only got 32 percent. When you translate that into dollars, you're also throwing away money." He uses Milorganite, a product from Milwaukee based on dried, disinfected sewage sludge (www.milorganite.com). He applies it with a sprayer, as he does, alternately, the nitrogen-rich granules of methylene urea or those of IBDU, isobutylidene diurea. "To me IBDU is one of the best slow-release products that you can buy, but it is also the most expensive. I do get the brown patch on my lawn, but I don't put chemicals down to control. I try to use good fertility and water management."

New and Natural

One of the newest guides from the University of Missouri Extension is a twelve-page manual called *Natural Lawn Care—* guide G6749. It starts by acknowledging that "increasing numbers of homeowners are inquiring about low-impact environmental approaches to lawn care." It continues with discussions of carbohydrate-based fertilizers—of vegetable or animal meal, of composted food waste or manure—and how they help sustain a healthy soil. Corn gluten as an organic fertilizer, it says, also may help control the emergence of grassy and broadleaf weeds. It lists more than a dozen products by brand name or type. And it details disease and insect management using organic and preventive methods. As always in good gardening, it suggests getting a soil test first—by taking a dozen random cores, each 4 inches deep with a trowel or shovel, around the lawn, removing any plant materials and taking the dried soil to the county extension office, where it's sent to an MU lab for testing. Also recommended is MU publication G6954, *Soil Testing for Lawns.* Finally, it advises that natural lawn care is a long-term not short-term process, but worth it for many reasons, including this, in a summary: "Protecting surface and groundwater quality is a serious environmental issue."

Have some antilawn tendencies and want to join folks who don't like to spew pollution into the air by mowing all summer long? Any time you're brave enough to take out your turf and plant appealing ground covers, consider these plants:

- A sweep of the low-growing Missouri Plant of Merit emeritus *Epimedium* x *versicolor* 'Sulphureum' for shade

Timing Is Everything

Fertilize. Hands down, fall is the time to fertilize cool-season grasses, either with an organic or a synthetic product. Plant growth is slowing down. And cool-season turf, like other plants, tends to store up rather than directly use the nitrogen it takes from soil in the fall and so it's not putting out excessive aboveground growth. If the bulk of fertilizing is done in spring, cool-season grasses grow unnaturally fast and are more susceptible to disease. The warm-season zoysia, on the other hand, should be fertilized from May through August; applications done too early in spring promote premature growth on top before roots get going and also benefit weeds.

Water when turf needs it. Rules of thumb are at least one thorough watering a week—an inch or so, monitored by an inexpensive rain gauge, if needed. To help ward off disease, water early in the morning so that blades of grass have time to dry.

Mow grass when it needs it. Best cutting heights for cool-season, turf-type tall fescue are between 3 and 4 inches; for bluegrass, from 2½ to 3½ inches. Lawn cut taller helps shade ground, conserves moisture, and helps the grass compete more successfully with weeds. Cutting heights for warm-season grass may range from 1½ to 2½ inches. And to reduce the stress that mowing causes turf, keep the mower's blade sharp and—in high heat—mow late in the day.

- The low-growing grass *Liriope* in sun or part shade, with the green and white *L. muscari* 'Variegata' staying put where it's planted, while the all-green *L. spicata* spreads
- For native lovers: wild ginger (*Asarum canadense*), a dream in shade because weeds don't grow under its own little canopy of deep green leaves

Garden
Solutions

Coping with Invasive Plants, Pests, and Diseases

Invasive plants may be among the newest concerns for Missouri home gardeners. Seminars and meetings on the subject are packed with people who want to understand what damage bush honeysuckle, lespedeza, or purple loosestrife may do to their yards and neighboring environments. But plant-chomping pests and disfiguring diseases also are perennial problems for gardeners of all stripes. Many such concerns find their way into questions for master gardeners, extension offices, and horticulture phone lines around the state.

These days integrated pest management (IPM) also is the new catchphrase for anyone hoping to control pests—invasives, insects, and diseases—in an environmentally responsible manner. So before we discuss strategies for handling individual pests, let's first look at this IPM approach and see what it can do for you.

Integrated Pest Management

Consider the concept of integrated pest management before applying a pesticide or fungicide. Initially developed for farmers and other growers by the U.S. Environmental Protection Agency, IPM is a four-step process that is easily applied to home gardens as well. It includes: 1) defining a point at which a pest needs controlling—more than one sighting, for instance; 2) clearly identifying the insects or weeds in question, so as to rule out the use of pesticides if not needed; 3) preventing problems in the first place, and in a cost-effective way, by rotating crops, selecting pest-resistant varieties, planting pest-free rootstock, or all of the above; 4) once a pest is identified as broadly affecting plants, using the least risky controls first—"highly targeted chemicals, such as pheromones to disrupt pest mating," says an EPA guideline, "or mechanical control, such as trapping or weeding." If less risky controls are not working, "then additional pest control methods would be employed, such as targeted spraying of pesticides. Broadcast spraying of nonspecific pesticides is a last resort." See www.epa.gov/pesticides/factsheets/ipm.htm for more of this information. Or sign up for an IPM online newsletter by the University of Missouri at http://ipm.missouri.edu. Or refine your approach with fact sheets from the Missouri Botanical Garden, including one promoting "the judicious use of chemical pesticides applied at the most vulnerable time in an insect's life history" (visit www.mobot.org/gardeninghelp/plantfinder/pests.shtml).

What Is an Invasive Plant?

An invader is a nonnative plant—not existing in Missouri before European settlement—and one that threatens the state's native biodiversity. There are thousands of exotic plants that get shipped into midwestern markets and sold by garden centers each year. "Most exotic plants are not pests and not a problem," says Tiffany Knight, assistant professor of biology at Washington University in St. Louis. But when exotics are bad for the environment, they are very, very bad, indeed. Take garlic mustard, or poor man's mustard (*Alliaria petiolata*). It is an herb with coarsely toothed leaves and buttonlike clusters of small white flowers that was introduced in the United States in the 1880s from Europe for food and medicinal use. Today it has escaped into woods in more than half of the country, including all of the Midwest. It is relentless in crowding out native species, says Knight. "Where there are fifty native understory species normally in woodland areas," she says, "when those areas are dominated by garlic mustard, there are few native understory plants. And tree seedlings get outcompeted where garlic mustard grows. People worry about Missouri's oaks in this regard."

Invasive Plants in Missouri

While garlic mustard is not a pretty garden plant and is not sold in garden centers, there are other invasive plants that either look like good garden companions or that still are found in retail settings. The Missouri Department of Conservation and the Missouri Botanical Garden have taken a lead in identifying exotic pest plants that are invading yards, gardens, and woodland settings across the state. Look to www.mdc.mo.gov or to www.mobot.org and search for "invasive plants" or "exotic pest plants." Also, check out Weeds Gone Wild, a Web site by the U.S. government, at www.nps.gov/plants/alien. George Yatskievych adds a caveat. "One additional point that should be important to gardeners," says Yatskievych, director of the Flora of Missouri Project at the Missouri Botanical Garden, "is that the same species that are escaping into the wild to become invasive exotics also are usually aggressive in the garden, either coming up everywhere from seed or growing so aggressively as to overtake other plants."

Here are just a few Missouri invaders, starting with two that are extremely prevalent in the state:

Japanese honeysuckle (*Lonicera japonica*). This twining, vining plant with classic white honeysuckle flowers—as tubes, each split into a spray of petals—was brought to this country as a ground cover. It clings and chokes plants as well as shades out natives and other desirable plants. It's one of several *Lonicera* species that spurred formation of the Gateway Honeysuckle Consortium for learning about and disposing of invasive honeysuckle, especially on public lands in the St. Louis area. A best way for the home gardener to dispose of this plant is the IPM way— regular weeding, so that these plants don't get a foothold in the garden. But on established Japanese honeysuckle, the remedy may be cutting it back but leaving some foliage on which is carefully painted a short-lived herbicide containing glyphosate—such as Roundup—that's absorbed through the leaves to kill the plant's roots. Timing is everything. If using herbicides, do so safely and especially in the fall when, says Yatskievych, "the plants are translocating nutrients into the roots for storage; that is when Roundup infiltrates the root system best."

Sericea or Chinese lespedeza (*Lespedeza cuneata*) was brought into this country not as a garden plant but for erosion control. It quickly moved into fields and disturbed areas beyond roadsides. It's now a threat to prairies, open woodlands, wetland borders, and meadows. Growing to between 3 and 5 feet tall, with alternate leaves on spiny stems, it may crowd out natives and ensure that there's an extensive seed bank of this plant in the soil. A high tannin content in leaves and stems makes it unpalatable to native wildlife.

The following invasives are found in at least ten Missouri counties, according to a working list of exotic pest plants by research staff at the Missouri Botanical Garden:

Autumn olive (*Elaeagnus umbellata*) is an Asian native once sold as a garden plant as well as for erosion control. That is, "until people started to get really concerned," says Tiffany Knight. The shrub may grow to 20 feet tall. Birds eat its fleshy fruit and spread the seeds. It may be found far from planting sites—along roadsides, in pastures, in fields, and on edges of woodland. A native to China, Korea, and Japan, it's now taken up unwanted residence in many parts of Missouri. A good way to recognize this plant is by its silver- to rust-colored scales on twigs and leaves.

Bush honeysuckle (*Lonicera maackii*). In a slide presentation and talk to more than two hundred people on a recent St. Louis winter evening, Tiffany Knight estimated that she sees bush honeysuckle in "75 percent of the yards" that she passes on the MetroLink light-rail system to and from Washington U. Bush honeysuckle is another exotic shrub that may grow to 15 feet in height and overshadow and kill any natives underneath. Older stems are hollow and help distinguish this plant from certain native honeysuckles. "Take out an old bush honeysuckle and you see nothing and probably no seeds in the soil waiting to come back. If the shrub hasn't been there for too long, you will see a flush of native plants return." One approach to eliminating this invasive is to cut it back and apply a short-lived herbicide to the stump (see Japanese honeysuckle, above).

Kudzu (*Pueraria montana* var. *lobata*) is an extremely invasive perennial vine that was used in the southeastern United States—and in Missouri—for erosion control long before its aggressive nature was known. Its twining vines create canopies and choke out other plants. "Efforts to control kudzu infestations have included the following methods: cutting, grazing, digging, disking, prescribed burning, and application of herbicides," says a report on the Missouri Department of Conservation's Web site www.mdc.mo.gov. Go there and search "kudzu" for details on various IPM treatments timed to the plant's life cycle.

Purple loosestrife (*Lythrum salicaria*) is a perennial that clogs ditches, pond edges, reservoirs, and other waterways in northeastern and some midwestern states and also is on Missouri's official "noxious weeds" list. However, some gardeners still demand it for its tall spikes and unflagging purple color in summer heat. And so a few Missouri garden centers continue to carry it. The argument that the market only sells sterile cultivars of purple loosestrife doesn't wash, according to the experts. "Some of these cultivars have just reduced sterility," says Knight. "It isn't safe to use them, especially if they hybridize with wild plants." *Noxious Weeds of Missouri,* available online at http://extension.missouri .edu/explore/agguides/pest/ipm1014.htm, has many details on pest plants. Says Yatskievych, "It is important to note that the law does not discriminate among different kinds of purple loosestrife. It states that the import and sale of *L. salicaria*, including all hybrids and cultivars, is illegal." He recalls an attempt in recent years by the Missouri Department of Conservation to eradicate purple loosestrife from a wetland area "with the owner's permission. That went on for several years and eventually involved hundreds of sites in about twenty-five counties. It was abandoned as ineffective," he adds, "because plants came back from seeds at existing infestations and new ones continued to be added. Eventually, the program simply could not keep up with the demand."

Wintercreeper (found in garden centers as *Euonymus fortunei*, now also classified as *E. hederaceus*) was introduced from China in the early 1900s as a fast-growing ground cover, and is still sold as such. New cultivars may be touted as less invasive. But in several states it is seen as a threat to native plants because of its ability to spread rapidly. "I've seen it in forested areas where it becomes really dominant," says Knight. "I don't think we know as much about it as we do garlic mustard. People should be wary of it."

Knight, a Florida native who does much of her work at Washington U's Tyson Research Center (www.biology.wustl.edu/ tyson), is impressed with the level of awareness of invasives in Missouri. "Environmentally, I think Missouri is very progressive," she says, "with the whole master gardener program and work at the botanical gardens. For the most part people have a real positive attitude about gardening with natives here, and that's really how it's going to change."

Elegant Substitutes for Invasives

Native plants may indeed be an answer, even in cultivated gardens. As just one example, think of lilac purple spikes of prairie blazing star (*Liatris pycnostachya*) instead of the slightly more reddish purple spires of invasive purple loosestrife (*Lythrum salicaria*). But don't rule out cultivars, such as a new pink *Veronica*, called 'Pink Damask', featuring long, upright spikes of tiny flowers that are the pastel image of *Lythrum* in July and August.

To replace torn-out, invasive bush honeysuckle (*Lonicera maackii*), consider the beautiful but underused—and slower growing—bottlebrush buckeye (*Aesculus parviflora*), a native to the southeastern United States and a Missouri Plant of Merit.

There are such polite replacements for vining Japanese honeysuckle as the red, trumpet-flowered honeysuckle (*Lonicera sempervirens*), termed a "well-behaved U.S. native" with "nonstop blooms," on the Plants of Merit listing, with at least one St. Louis–area garden center—Cottage Garden (www.cottgardens .com)—boasting new cultivars of *L. sempervirens*, such as 'Alabama Crimson' and 'Major Wheeler'.

For other ideas, look for the books *Native Alternatives to Invasive Plants*, by C. Colston Burrell, from the Brooklyn Botanic Garden's All-Region Guides, and *Tried and True Missouri Native Plants for Your Yard*, published by the Missouri Department of Conservation.

Plant Pests in Missouri

Before rushing to spray or dust plants for possible insect infestation, go through the IPM steps and rule out any environmental causes. A case in point is the annual deluge of calls to Missouri gardening hotlines in late June and July about sunken brown patches on the blossom ends of tomatoes and peppers. The culprit is inconsistent moisture in soil, not pests. Blossom-end rot is the name of this condition. "They always want to know what to spray," says St. Louis Master Gardener Ronda Anson of the people who call the Missouri Botanical Garden Answer Service. "What you spray is water. Once a week you water tomatoes and keep them mulched. It's that uneven watering that causes calcium deficiencies that cause blossom-end rot. And it's not a calcium deficiency in the soil. Tomatoes only take up calcium from the soil with water."

Insects: The Good, the Bad, and the Ugly

Good bugs are also called beneficials. These are the ladybugs and lacewings that eat aphids, whiteflies, mites, and other bugs doing damage to plants. Microscopic nematodes—the good type that go after ants, fleas, cutworms, and more than two hundred soil-dwelling pests—also feast on the grubs that do damage to lawns before morphing into flower-chomping Japanese beetles. Beneficials in another sense—those that pollinate—are bees, butterflies, and wasps. Even—or especially—the lowly earthworm benefits the garden by aerating soil and depositing castings that decompose and help add nutrients to the earth. It's important to take all of these creatures into consideration and to go through your IPM checklist before spraying with insecticides that are likely to kill both good and bad.

They may serve a purpose in nature, but bad bugs can cause seemingly endless problems for the home gardener. Here are just a few.

Aphids. These tiny plant-eating insects show up most often on new growth, eating sap in the stems and sometimes transmitting plant viruses. A strong spray of water should wash them off.

Predatory insects—the beneficial ladybugs, for instance—also help keep aphids in check. Mature plants and trees tend to survive aphid attacks. Younger plants may need extra attention, such as regular washings with water before a decision to spray with insecticidal soap—such as ones made from potassium salts of fatty acids that work to dry out the waxy outer skins of insects. Neem oil (extracted from the neem tree, a native of India) also interrupts insect growth patterns. Read labels carefully before purchase and use, especially of any broad-spectrum products.

Japanese beetles. They could be the top candidate for "ugly." These little black green iridescent insects cluster on garden flowers in early summer. "Some years are worse than others for Japanese beetles," says St. Louis Master Gardener Ronda Anson, who has picked off her fair share of the slow-moving adult beetles and dropped them in soapy water—very IPM. But since she's educated neighbors against using the beetle traps—ones that actually draw more beetles to an area—"they've been a minor pest. They do like irrigated turf," she adds, "because it's easier for them to drill into moist soil." Neem oil also may be considered a treatment; be sure to follow label directions.

Mites. Their numbers soar in Missouri's hottest weather. "Watch for webbing on plants, indicating mite damage (mites love this weather)," says a recent heat-wave advisory e-mailed to members of the Missouri Botanical Garden. "Typical mite victims," it continues, "are Alberta spruce, cotoneaster, honey locust, tomato, burning bush, and marigolds." Washing them off with water is a nontoxic approach. Insecticidal soap used frequently is another. "If applying chemicals for control of pests, diseases, or weeds," the advisory says, "wait until the temperatures are below 90 degrees Fahrenheit and there is no wind. It is best to wait until morning hours to get this done. Heat and pesticides/herbicides may drift with high heat vapors into nearby plantings. Also, heat and chemicals can become toxic to plant leaves." With any use of pesticides, label directions should be read and carefully followed.

Scale insects affect shrubs, trees, succulents, fruits, and indoor plants. They are tiny, rounded pests that leave a sticky "honeydew" substance on leaves that, in turn, may become blackened with mold. Spray affected deciduous trees with dormant oil in winter. And always spray patio plants with insecticidal soap before bringing them into the house each fall. Other, stronger sprays may be needed for severe infestations. Following label directions is essential.

Thrips, like spider mites, thrive in hot, dry conditions. Adult thrips are tiny brownish black insects with narrow bodies, while immature nymphs are yellow orange. Both feed on the upper surfaces of leaves. "They tend to like pale-colored flowers," says Ronda Anson, of her garden. Pale-colored roses, oleander, dahlia, daylilies, and peonies are commonly attacked by thrips. "But an attack doesn't kill the plant," Anson says. Reduce heat stress in the garden with regular watering. Consider sprayings with insecticidal soap if thrips do serious damage. As always, follow label directions.

Sod webworms are increasingly common problems for Missouri lawns. Damage is worst in drought as well as to newly established turf. The moths of sod webworms are active late in the day, and if large numbers are observed, a gardener may wait a few days to mix an ounce or two of dishwashing detergent in a gallon of water and spread over a small patch of lawn. Larvae should come to the surface. These larvae are prized by many beneficial predators but may require further treatment if they're too prevalent.

Tent caterpillars create large white nests spun in the branches of many deciduous trees. Many birds feed on the hairy black caterpillars that also have blue spots and white lines down their backs. This pest is more of a nuisance and cosmetic problem than a threat to tree health, unless full-scale defoliation occurs. Look for eggs on smaller branches in late winter and prune off those branches or, later, remove young nests completely. Some experts also recommend applying mineral oil to kill eggs.

Whiteflies attack flowers, vegetables, and fruit, indoors and out, and are difficult pests to control, especially since there are some pesticide-resistant strains around. As with scale, whiteflies excrete a sticky substance on leaves. Unlike scale, whitefly is characterized by small white insects flying off of plants when disturbed. Careful spraying with insecticidal soaps is encouraged—following label directions—before bringing a plant into the house for winter.

Furry Pests: Moles, Voles, Rabbits, and Deer

Moles generally are harmless, says St. Louis Master Gardener Ronda Anson. But she fields dozens of calls about them anyway in her volunteer work for the Missouri Botanical Garden's Horticulture Answer Service. "They can kill plants, but really what they do more than anything else is eat insects underground. The problem with moles is more of a cosmetic one with the tunnels." Voles, on the other hand, live aboveground as much as underneath and eat plants just as rabbits do, preferring foliage, flowers, seeds as well as the bark of young fruit trees. Trapping voles or repelling them with hot pepper sprayed onto plants is one of Anson's suggestions, as is keeping vegetation away from the bases of trees, brush cleared, and grass mowed to no taller than 4 inches. Ridding yards of rabbits includes a similar clean-up, although there is enough knowledge about what rabbits—and deer—do not like to eat to plant a pest-resistant garden. Go to www.gardeninghelp.org and search "rabbits" and "deer' for extensive lists of plants that these pests hate, as well as for nontoxic repellants for use in Missouri gardens. Finally, consider fencing the animals out. Go to http://extension.missouri.edu and, again, search "rabbits" and "deer" for new fence ideas.

Plant Diseases and Disorders in Missouri

It's possible to reduce the impact that plant diseases have on home gardens by keeping tools, stakes, and other garden equipment clean; by ensuring that soil is fertile and that its structure is loose; and by selecting disease-resistant plant varieties in the first place. Even with all of that, disease sometimes hits.

Alternaria, or early blight, is something that you do not want your tomato plants to get. And yet spores of this fungus may live in your soil, on old plant debris, even on tomato cages. The blight generally begins as tiny spots on lower leaves, progressing upward and even defoliating plants. Controls include rotating tomatoes to different soils in the garden each year, keeping the plants well-mulched to prevent spores in soil from splashing up on lower leaves, using disease-resistant varieties such as 'Jetstar' and 'Supersonic', and disinfecting tools and tomato supports.

Dogwood anthracnose is a fungal disease that has caused serious losses among flowering dogwoods in landscapes across the eastern and southern United States. So far, Missouri's native dog-woods (*Cornus florida*) have not suffered this fate, although anthracnose has been found on some nursery stock in the state. Symptoms include leaf spots and blotches, twig and branch dieback, cankers, and the death of the tree. Managing the disease includes reducing shade; watering in dry months; destroying infected trees; and planting ones that are resistant, including the relatively resistant *C. kousa, C. racemosa, C. canadensis, C. alternifolia,* and *C. mas.*

Fire blight is a bacterial disease that affects pear trees, apples, cotoneasters, and hawthorns. The trees and shrubs develop cankers on branches, leaves shrivel and turn brown, and the entire plant may die. Remove affected plants or prune at least 2 feet past a damaged area and disinfect pruners, or saws, between cuts.

Leaf spot of the fungal variety occurs on many different plants, most famously on roses but also on tomatoes. Because fungal spores of black spot germinate in the spring from diseased fallen leaves and canes and are disseminated by splashing water, a good remedy is to remove all affected parts of a plant and rake up and discard any fallen leaves. Also contact a local rosarian—via the American Rose Society's list on www.ars.org—for names of disease-resistant varieties. Septoria leaf spot of tomato also is a fungus, producing smaller spots in conditions of high humidity for long stretches of time. Controls are similar to ones for leaf spot of roses: removing diseased leaves from plants and from the ground; improving air circulation around plants; mulching at the base; and watering at the base, not from overhead.

Powdery mildew "is a huge problem in Missouri," says Anson, "because of our humidity. Everything gets it, from oaks to bee balm, phlox, zinnias, and lilacs." Its symptoms are a white powdery fungal growth on leaves. "We're seeing it on a lot of stuff we haven't seen it on in the past," says Anson, siting problems with air circulation and too much shade. "Lilacs are easy to grow here, if they're given full sun and good air circulation. People keep trying to put them in shade, and they don't tolerate that at all."

Rose rosette is a disfiguring disease that looks much like a witch's broom—with elongated shoots and small distorted leaves. It is spread by tiny airborne mites. It's impossible to prevent and, if found, should be treated by digging out and destroying the entire plant, roots and all. The exotic multiflora rose, first introduced in the United States from Japan, now is a noxious weed in Missouri and is credited with harboring rose rosette.

Rusts affect trees, shrubs, perennials, and annuals, giving affected plants small bright orange or brown patches on the undersides of their leaves and, in worst cases, pustules that appear to be bursting from within stems. Rusts are fungi, with spores spread by wind and splashing rain. Most rusts have two generations per season—the first on apples, for example, the second on junipers. Names such as cedar-apple rust, cedar-hawthorn rust, and cedar-quince rust represent the two hosts required to complete rust life cycles. Of the three, cedar-quince rust has the broadest effect on other plants, including roses. Before spraying, consider removal of one of the host plants.

Scab, too, is a fungal disease. Pears and crab apples, pyracanthas, and citrus get scab, with dark greenish brown patches on foliage that are scabby, sometimes blistered. Control with disease-resistant varieties, pruning to keep plants open in the center, and raking and discarding of all fallen leaves. Spraying, again, is a last resort, with the careful choice of product.

Where to Learn More

To get answers about invasives, pests, and diseases, there are many services around the state.

- The oldest is the Missouri Botanical Garden's Horticulture Answer Service, staffed for more than forty years by horticulturists and St. Louis Master Gardeners on weekdays from 9:00 a.m. to noon. Call (314) 577-5143.

- Consider taking a sample of a sick plant to master gardeners at the "Plant Doctor" desk—a walk-in service at the Missouri Botanical Garden, 4344 Shaw Boulevard, St. Louis 63110—and its Kemper Center for Home Gardening. Hours are 10:00 a.m. to 3:00 p.m. Monday through Saturday.
- Master Gardeners of Greater Kansas City answer gardening questions; phone the hotline at (816) 833-8733 weekdays 9:00 a.m. to 3:00 p.m. from March 1 to October 31. From November through February, questions left on the hotline's answering machine—also (816) 833-8733—get answered once a week.
- Master Gardeners of Greene County (Springfield) operate an informational hotline—at (417) 862-9284, ext. 18—to answer questions about lawn and garden. The hotline is staffed weekdays 8:30 a.m. to 4:30 p.m. from March through October. "During the 'off season,' November through February, you may leave a voice message," says an online notice, "and a Master Gardener will return the call within a day or two."
- Meanwhile, the University of Missouri Extension's Web editors and specialists take gardening questions online. Go to the Web site at http://extension.missouri.edu, hit the Contact button, and write up your question for possible publication—with answer—on the site. Some questions even may get you a direct response from editors.
- Another online source is the Missouri Botanical Garden's www.gardeninghelp.org site, with a new collection of answers to 1,700 topical gardening questions by a well-known St. Louis–area horticulturist. Go there, click on Questions and Answers by Chip Tynan! and search your topic.

CHAPTER ELEVEN

Learning from Missouri's Public Plantings

Missouri has a wealth of public gardens, parks, display plantings, and special gardening events that are open to the public and are great places to pick up fresh, new gardening ideas. Here is a sampling from around the state.

Public Gardens

EarthWays Center, in midtown St. Louis, is a new-tech environmental experience built into a quintessential St. Louis brick, Victorian home. Think Judy Garland in *Meet Me in St. Louis* and you're there, at 3617 Grandel Square, St. Louis 63108; (314) 577-0220. But for the new-tech part, go green, and sustainably so, to www.earthwayscenter.org. It's now a division of the Missouri Botanical Garden. You'll learn about native-plant landscaping, water- and energy-saving green-roof systems, and recycled-plastic lumber garden beds. And that's just on the outside. Actor/environmentalist Ed Begley Jr. would love the green home that it is indoors. Group tours are by appointment, and public tours happen on the third Saturday and Sunday of each month; admission is $3 per person, free to Missouri Botanical Garden members and children age twelve and under.

Jefferson Farm & Gardens. Go to www.jeffersonfarm.org to learn about contemporary Midwest farming and gardening on a new sixty-seven-acre educational farm located near the University of Missouri at 4800 New Haven Road, Columbia 65201. It is inspired by Thomas Jefferson's personal garden at Monticello and is to open to the public beginning in late summer 2008. "Americans have become increasingly disconnected from the sources of their food," says Rob Myers, executive director of the institute, "with most individuals at least two or three generations removed from a family farm member." Spending time on a farm "can get people thinking more about food production and can even help children make healthier choices in their foods, going for more fresh fruits and vegetables and less processed food." Admission is to be $5 for ages eighteen to sixty-four, $3 for ages two to seventeen and age sixty-five and above. For more information contact the Thomas Jefferson Agricultural Institute, 601 West Nifong Boulevard, Suite 1D, Columbia 65203; (573) 449-3518; www.jeffersoninstitute.org.

Kauffman Garden—with a full name of the Ewing and Muriel Kauffman Memorial Garden—is an intensely planted, exquisite two-acre urban garden right in the middle of Kansas City, near Country Club Plaza. It is free to the public and open daily 8:00 a.m. to dusk at 4800 Rockhill Road, Kansas City 64110. Staffers from Powell Gardens plant and maintain some seven thousand plants representing more than three hundred varieties. For more information call (816) 932-1200 or go to www.powell gardens.org/default.asp?page=kauffmanmap.

Missouri Botanical Garden is almost too big a horticulture source to catalog here. But key features are its intensely planted, and labeled, gardens at 4344 Shaw Boulevard, St. Louis 63110. This is the former "country" home of garden founder Henry Shaw. Within the botanical garden are Japanese and English gardens; rose gardens; the geodesic-domed Climatron for tropicals; collections of daylilies, irises, bulbs, and conifers; plus other installations of perennials that are part of the learning institution that is the Kemper Center for Home Gardening. Kemper's grounds feature display beds that include a new Plants of Merit garden. There's also a "Plant Doctor" desk and a gardening library inside Kemper. Volunteers at the desk will accept soil samples to be mailed off to labs for testing. Many of the botanical garden's seasonal classes for adults take place at Kemper. Go to www.mobot.org and click on Gardening and Classes for more information. Or call the recorded phone line at (314) 577-9400 or (800) 642-8842 for special events happening around the time that you want to visit. Admission is $8 for adults age thirteen and up, $5 for St. Louis City and County residents, free for garden members and children age twelve and under; admission for children at a new Children's Garden is $3, but for adults it's free.

Missouri Prairie Foundation is less a public garden and more of a conservation organization, helping to preserve and restore nearly three thousand acres of fast-disappearing tallgrass prairie at a number of locations. Educational materials are in the works. But already foundation members get beautiful quarterly *Prairie Journals* and the opportunity to camp on prairie land and help remove encroaching brush while learning other prairie-restoration techniques. For information about membership write to P.O. Box 200, Columbia, MO 65205; call (888) 843-6739; or visit www.moprairie.org.

Mizzou Botanic Garden in Columbia, literally, is the campus of the University of Missouri (Mizzou is the university's nickname, pronounced mah-ZOO). The campus landscape-services department features Tree Trails, with hundreds of labeled specimens detailed in a twenty-five-page color brochure, encouraging many lovely tree walks. Call (573) 882-4240 for more information or to request the Tree Trails brochure. Also get a Mizzou Botanic Garden map for finding the campus butterfly garden, hydrangea and daylily collections, perennial phlox and peony gardens, as well as a native Missouri tree collection, some of them "underrepresented on campus and seldom seen in the urban landscape," says the brochure. And there's a campus tribute to Missouri's Plants of Merit program, which promotes flowering perennials, annuals, shrubs, and trees that perform consistently well in gardens around the state. Go to http://gardens.missouri .edu for more on that. For more help contact the Office of Visitor Relations, 104 Jesse Hall, Columbia 65211; (800) 856-2181. Or e-mail visitus@missouri.edu.

Overland Park Arboretum and Botanical Gardens is just across the Missouri state line that plows through the Kansas City area, on three hundred acres of southern Johnson County. Most of the property is "dedicated to the preservation and restoration of natural ecosystems," says a mission statement, with the remainder including traditional botanical gardens. For more information write to the mailing address of 8909 West 179th Street, Overland Park, KS 66221; call (913) 685-3604; or go to www.opkansas.org. There is no admission fee.

Powell Gardens. The sky is as much a part of this 915-acre, prairielike space as are intensely planted perennial and annual beds, all near a contemporary, prairie-style visitor center. But there's also a spectacular Island Garden surrounded by water features in a large lake. Otherwise, paths through lovely parklike open areas prevail—that is, until you get to the new twelve-acre Heartland Harvest Garden—opening at apple-blossom time in spring 2009—with an Apple Celebration Court showcasing Missouri varieties,  plus four large quilt-pattern gardens—when viewed from above—that contain fruits, berries, home-garden vegetables, flowers, and herbs, among other edibles. This Kansas City–area botanical garden is located at 1609 Northwest U.S. Highway 50, Kingsville 64061. For more information call (816) 697-2600 or visit www.powellgardens.org. Admission from April to October is $8 for adults, $7 for senior citizens, $3 for children ages five to twelve, and free for children under age five and for Friends of Powell Gardens. Admission from November to March is $6 for adults, $5 for senior citizens, $2 for children ages five to twelve, and free for children under age five and for Friends of Powell Gardens.

Shaw Nature Reserve operates on 2,500 acres of Ozark landscape and includes trails through extensive prairie and woodland, as well as a Whitmire Wildflower Garden and, near the entrance, a fifty-five-acre expanse of meadows planted with conifers and thousands of daffodils blooming in spring. It is located southwest of St. Louis at the intersection of Missouri Highway 100 and Interstate 44, Gray Summit 63039, and is now also a division of the Missouri Botanical Garden. Call (636) 451-3512 or visit www.shawnature.org for more information. Admission is $3 for adults, $2 for seniors, free for children age twelve and under and for botanical garden members.

Sophia M. Sachs Butterfly House and Education Center, at Faust Park in Chesterfield, is a not-for-profit organization established in 1995 "to foster a better understanding of butterflies and increase awareness of the natural habitat in which butterflies thrive." It is now a division of the Missouri Botanical Garden. In 2000 it added an outdoor garden called the Native Habitat. For more information write to 15193 Olive Boulevard, Chesterfield, MO 63017; call (636) 530-0076; or go to www.butterflyhouse .org. Admission is $6.00 for adults, $4.50 for seniors, $4.00 for children ages four to twelve, $3.00 for botanical garden members at senior to sponsorship levels, and free to children age three and under and for upper-level garden members.

Truman State University and its new Gaber Solar Clock Garden is on the campus—at Patterson and Franklin Streets, near the administration building at 100 East Normal Street, in Kirksville 63501. This planting of annuals and perennials that bloom by time of day, from 8:00 a.m. to 6:00 p.m., but also seasonally, is a botany project of the university's science division. Go to http://solarclockgarden.truman.edu information.

Public Parks

Forest Park, at more than 1,200 acres, is the largest St. Louis City park and one of the largest urban parks in the country. It was home to the 1904 Louisiana Purchase Exposition that drew more than twenty million visitors from around the world. The park boasts beautifully landscaped areas around the St. Louis Zoo; the Muny, an outdoor summer theater; a refurbished river with new native wetlands and prairies; and the Jewel Box—an art deco glass conservatory with outdoor grounds tended by dedicated volunteer gardeners. For more information go to http://stlouis.missouri.org/ citygov/parks/forestpark or call the Department of Parks, Recreation and Forestry at (314) 289-5300.

Loose Park in Kansas City is home to public plantings around a lake, tennis courts, and picnic areas but is known most famously for its Laura Conyers Smith Municipal Rose Garden. The Loose Park Garden Center, meanwhile, was built in 1957 for garden-club meetings and horticultural exhibitions of all kinds. A library and garden-center grounds, at 5200 Pennsylvania Avenue, Kansas City 64112, are open to the public. Call (816) 784-5300 for more information or go to www.kcmo.org and search Loose Park. Established just a year shy of the facility is the Garden Center Association of Greater Kansas City, with a mission "to promote and encourage among citizens of the greater Kansas City area an interest in horticulture and related gardening activities." Visit www.gardencenterassociation.org for its many sponsored gardening events.

Nathanael Greene Park & Close Memorial Park at 2400 South Scenic Avenue, Springfield 65807, features a growing number of botanical interests, including a beautifully planted display garden of flowering perennials, herbs, espaliered apples, and other plants of interest to the home gardener, tended by Master Gardeners of Southwest Missouri and Greene County Extension and free to the public; and the Mizumoto Stroll Garden, a seven-acre Japanese garden, open April through October 9:00 a.m. to 7:30 p.m., with a $3 admission charge for adults. For more information about these and other area gardens, call (417) 864-1049 or go to www.springfieldmo.org.

Phelps Grove Park at 1200 East Bennett Street in Springfield 65804, is a forty-four-acre park containing the Springfield Art Museum, rose gardens, and a xeriscape garden exhibit. For more information visit www.springfieldmo.org.

Tower Grove Park in St. Louis was given to the city in 1868 by the founder of the nearby Missouri Botanical Garden, Henry Shaw. It features more than eight thousand mature trees and shrubs that Shaw imported from around the world. Brightly painted Victorian pavilions also fill park land. And in front of the recently restored

When to . . . *see gardens on tour*

Spring and summer plant festivals and garden tours abound in Missouri. Plant societies and garden clubs are key sponsors of these events (see "Resources," chapter 12). But so are botanical gardens. For instance, eight to ten of the top home gardens in the St. Louis area open to the public every three years for a daylong bus tour, plus box lunch, coordinated by the Missouri Botanical Garden's membership office. Go to www.mobot.org and click on Membership or Member Events for dates and costs. The public is welcome on all of these tours. Master gardeners also organize terrific home-garden tours (look in chapter 12 under "MU—University of Missouri Extension"). And don't overlook displays and plant and seed sales at the small-town fairs and festivals, such as Mansfield's Baker Creek Heirloom Seeds spring festival (http://rareseeds.com) as well as Charleston's annual Dogwood-Azalea Festival, tour, and plant sale (www.charleston mo.org/festival).

Piper Palm House are the Lily Ponds, where Victorian-inspired water lilies grow. For more information call (314) 771-2679 or log on to http://stlouis.missouri.org/parks /tower-grove. The park is located at 4256 Magnolia Avenue, St. Louis 63110.

Watkins Woolen Mill State Park and State Historic Site in Clay County, northeast of Kansas City, features an exquisite heirloom garden of vegetable, fruit, herb, and flower varieties that were available to home gardeners prior to 1880. They are part of the site's "living history program" and are planted in raised beds as well as open plots of vegetables surrounded by herb and flower borders. Master gardeners tend the garden. For more information call the state park at (816) 580-3387 or go online to www.mostateparks.com/wwmill/garden.htm. When visiting the site, at 26600 Park Road North, Lawson 64062, also pick up a list of sources for heirloom seed.

Display Plantings

A trademarked slogan for the not-for-profit group called All-America Selections is "Tested Nationally and Proven Locally." This means that annual flowers and vegetables are tested in a network of AAS trial and display gardens around the country before a few of these plants are picked as best for home gardens each year. In Missouri there are a number of sites where AAS winners are on display to the public, according to the AAS at www.all-america selections.org. These include gardens at Southeast Missouri State University, 1039 Bertling Street, Cape Girardeau 63701; University of Missouri, Department of Horticulture, on the grounds of the university turf farm, 3600 New Haven Road, Columbia 65201; Loose Park Garden Center, 5200 Pennsylvania Avenue, Kansas City 64112; Missouri Botanical Garden, 4344 Shaw Boulevard, St. Louis 63110; Powell Gardens, 1609 Northwest U.S. Highway 50, Kingsville 64061; St. Louis Community College–Meramec Horticulture Department, 11333 Big Bend Boulevard, Kirkwood 63122; St. Louis County Parks Department's Jefferson Barracks Park, Laborer's House Garden, 533 Grant Road, St. Louis 63125; and Queeny Park Barn Courtyard, 1675 South Mason Road, St. Louis 63131.

CHAPTER TWELVE

Resources for the Missouri Gardener

Sharing knowledge with like-minded folks is one of the perks of being a gardener. There's nothing like visiting a spectacular butterfly garden at someone's Missouri home and leaving with plastic bags of free plants, not to mention new gardening ideas. Here are some groups around the state—from community gardens, garden clubs, plant societies, and sources of plants and seeds to gardening Web sites, government agencies, professional groups, and universities—all with lots of knowledge to share.

Community Gardens

Community Garden Coalition of Columbia and Boone County is a not-for-profit corporation supporting garden plots for the elderly and lower-income folks. "We help gardeners stretch their food dollar and improve their nutritional intake by growing their own vegetables," says a mission statement. Call (573) 875-5995 or go online to http://cgc.missouri.org.

    Gateway Greening, Inc., is a not-for-profit in the city of St. Louis, "dedicated to community development through community gardening." Since 1984 it has helped turn hundreds of abandoned lots into neighborhood gardens and landscaped oases. Its staff, master gardeners, and other volunteers also work to help beautify downtown. Call (314) 588-9600 or visit www.gateway greening.org.

Kansas City Community Gardens are headquartered in Swope Park at 6917 Kensington Avenue, where a store sells seeds to anyone who gardens there or at home. The mission is "to improve the quality of life of low-income households and other members of the community by helping them grow their own nutritious fruits and vegetables." Call (816) 931-3877 or go to www.kccg.org.

Garden Clubs

There are too many great garden clubs around the state to mention here. And so here are two umbrella groups representing hundreds of local clubs, plus a highly active category of clubs—ones that focus on water gardens.

Federated Garden Clubs of Missouri, Inc., represents ten separate gardening districts in the state. Go to www.gardenclubs ofmissouri.org for information on 145 garden clubs representing nearly three thousand members, who organize plant sales, meetings, and other local and regional events.

National Garden Clubs, Inc., is a St. Louis–based, not-for-profit educational organization composed of 6,500 garden clubs in fifty states and the District of Columbia, for a total of more than 200,000 members. It works to award college scholarships, to sponsor classes, and to "advance the study of gardening, landscape design, environmental issues, floral design, and horticulture." Call (314) 776-7574 or visit www.gardenclub.org.

Water Garden Society of Greater Kansas City, www.kcwatergardens.com, is one of the extremely active, private, not-for-profit gardening groups in the state, as is the **St. Louis Water Gardening Society,** at www.slwgs.org, both sponsoring annual tours and other events.

Gardening Web Sites

http://drought.unl.edu is for gardeners and for weather geeks, the site of a spectacular weekly update of drought across the country. This Drought Monitor Map is made possible by the folks at the National Drought Mitigation Center, at the University of Nebraska–Lincoln.

http://extension.missouri.edu/explore is a route to knowledge of many, if not all, things gardening—and farming—in the Show-Me State. The University of Missouri Extension keeps and updates extensive online files about every aspect of home gardening and landscaping from fruit to nuts to lawn and trees, and every plant and pest in between. Explore your way through the "explore" guides by clicking on Agriculture to get to gardening topics (see more about extension help under "Universities," below).

www.cocorahs.org is a volunteer network of weather watchers called the Community Collaborative Rain, Hail & Snow Network.

www.grownative.org is an innovative, joint program of the Missouri Department of Conservation (MDC) and the Missouri Department of Agriculture (MDA). Grow Native! promotes use of native plants with a Web site full of hundreds of color images of natives and clear descriptions of their best uses, helping to "protect and restore our state's biodiversity by increasing conservation awareness of native plants and their effective use by commercial landscapers as well as the home gardener."

www.heartlandtreealliance.org is the home to Heartland Tree Alliance, a Kansas City–area Web site with more information about trees and links to some of the dozens of other sites promoting good tree care and urban and community forestry.

www.missouriexchange.com is an online "place to buy and sell Missouri-produced products." The University of Missouri Center for Agroforestry, in cooperation with the Grow Native! program, started this innovative online marketplace in recent years "to increase business opportunities for native plant materials and Missouri alternative products." To date, native seeds, culinary herbs, fruits, and vegetables seem to be topping the list of salable items.

www.mobot.org is the Missouri Botanical Garden's Web site and perhaps the definitive gardening site in the state, with thirteen million page views a year, according to Glenn Kopp, designer and manager of PlantFinder, a site-within-the-site featuring photos and detailed information on some four thousand plants at the garden. A shortened address—www.gardeninghelp.org—takes

you to PlantFinder but also to a bloom-time chart for plants, updated weekly; to a Monthly Gardening Calendar for St. Louis; to some fifty fact sheets from the botanical garden's Kemper Center for Home Gardening; to more than 1,700 home-gardening questions fielded over recent years by the garden's senior horticulturist Chip Tynan, also manager of the garden's Horticulture Answer Service, (314) 577-5143, Monday through Friday, 9:00 a.m. to noon.

www.mocommunitytrees.com. The Missouri Community Forestry Council is composed of members from six regions of the state, meeting bimonthly in each region to discuss local tree management. For the homeowner this group's Web site has an extensive set of links to information on tree care, planting, and selection. There are also details on the group's latest strategies in its Missouri campaign against tree topping—a not-uncommon practice in some rural, as well as urban, areas. Topping, says the Web site, "is the drastic removal, or cutting back of large branches in mature trees, leaving large, open wounds which subject the tree to disease and decay."

www.ozarksgardens.com, a charming Web site featuring photos of southwest Missouri gardens by Springfield native Frank Shipe, a former professional gardener and landscaper as well as writer and editor. He also includes tidbits and observations about each garden, plus general gardening advice on soils and climate for areas in and around the Ozarks.

www.powellgardens.org for Powell Gardens, a private, not-for-profit botanical garden on more than nine hundred acres—once a dairy farm—just east of Kansas City. Besides established perennial gardens and a new, twelve-acre Heartland Harvest Garden, the Web site's "learn" section includes ever-changing classes, a catalog of plants on the grounds, and other Missouri-gardening links.

www.savvygardener.com may be the Kansas City area's favorite online resource for gardening, lawn, and landscape advice. Thousands of area gardeners read the online newsletter each week, according to the Web site. Among other gems are weekly gardening tips for the Kansas City area, weather conditions and weather alerts, plus "recommended action" for what makes Missouri gardening a challenge—"late freezes, droughts, excessive rain, and heat."

www.shawnature.org is a Web site packed with information on native plants and native landscaping from horticulturists at the 2,400-acre Shaw Nature Reserve. This division of the Missouri Botanical Garden is located at Gray Summit, about 30 miles southwest of St. Louis. Its site also details programs for adults and families—including overnights—and keeps an active calendar for such popular events as a spring wildflower sale, prairie day, and harvest festival.

Government Agencies

City of Kansas City (www.kcmo.org). Go there and search "gardening" for such Loose Park Garden Center events as programs by rosarians as well as by horticulturists from Powell Gardens. Or type "forestry" into the search field for ways to connect with urban foresters if you have questions about trees along streets or parkways. (In St. Louis click on Forestry at http://stlouis .missouri.org for this service.)

Missouri Department of Conservation (www.mdc.mo.gov) is the single most important state agency for imparting information on nature and native plants to citizens of the state. Besides the online advice given via its Grow Native! program—at www.grownative.org, in partnership with the Missouri Department of Agriculture—the conservation department sends out free gardening information, such as the publications *Missouri Urban Trees* and *Missouri Conservation Trees and Shrubs,* available by writing to Missouri Department of Conservation, P.O. Box 180, Jefferson City, MO 65102, or by e-mailing pubstaff@mdc.mo.gov. The department sells books and other items through its MDC Nature Shop: (877) 521-8632; www.mdcnatureshop.com. And the conservation department offers Missouri residents a variety of seedlings for reforestation, windbreaks, erosion control, as well as wildlife food and cover. Go to www.mdc.mo.gov/forest/nursery/ seedling for more information.

National Weather Service. Go to www.weather.gov for the home page, then click on your part of Missouri. However, the state's all-important precipitation analysis may be found at another great site, www.srh.noaa.gov/rfcshare/precip_analysis_ new.php.

Plant Societies

Search the Missouri Botanical Garden's Web site at www.mobot .org for updates on St. Louis–area plant society contacts listed here. For Kansas City updates, click on www.kcmo.org/parks for plant-society and garden-club events at the Loose Park Garden Center, 5200 Pennsylvania Avenue. But wherever you live in

Missouri, look for information about plant sales sponsored by such local groups. Members know what grows well in your area and are delighted to impart care-and-feeding information about their favorite specimens while selling them at bargain prices. If your society is not listed here, it's for reasons of space. But there is one worthy plant—the fern—that's not represented by a Missouri society and yet does have a St. Louis connection: George Yatskievych, membership secretary of the American Fern Society. Contact him or the society via the Web site http://amerfernsoc .org. Here are some other societies in the state:

Boxwood. The Boxwood Society of the Midwest is in St. Louis. Go to www.mobot.org and search "plant societies." For the American Boxwood Society, go directly to www.boxwood society.org.

Cacti. Get to the Henry Shaw Cactus Society (St. Louis) or the Kansas City Cactus & Succulent Society through the Web site of the Cactus & Succulent Society of America, www.cssainc.org.

Carnivorous plants. The St. Louis Carnivorous Plants Society is listed at www.mobot.org; search "plant societies." For the International Carnivorous Plant Society, go to www.carnivorous plants.org.

Daffodils. The Greater St. Louis Daffodil Society, along with many other pertinent daffodil facts, is on the site of the American Daffodil Society at http://daffodilusa.org.

Dahlias. The Greater St. Louis Dahlia Society's Web site is at www.stldahliasociety.com. For the Kansas City Dahlia Society, go through the American Dahlia Society site, www.dahlia.org.

Daylilies. For the many daylily societies throughout Missouri, go to the American Hemerocallis (Daylily) Society site at www.daylilies.org and click on Regional Activities.

Herbs. The St. Louis Herb Society is at www.stlouisherb society.com. Find the Webster Groves Herb Society and the St. Louis Evening Herbalists through www.mobot.org; search "plant societies." Greater Kansas City Herb Study Group meets monthly at Loose Park Garden Center; see www.kcmo.org/parks. The site of the Herb Society of America is www.herbsociety.org.

Hostas. The Greater Ozarks Hosta Society, the Heartland Hosta and Shade Plant Society, and St. Louis Hosta Society are all on the American Hosta Society site: www.hosta.org.

Irises. The Greater Kansas City Iris Society and Greater St. Louis Iris Society are two of nearly a dozen iris groups around the state; see the American Iris Society Web site at www.irises.org for information on these clubs.

Lilies. The Mid America (St. Louis) Regional Lily Society is at www.marls.org, while Ozark Regional Lily Society contacts and other lily events are on the site of the North American Lily Society, www.lilies.org.

Natives. Go to the site of the North American Native Plant society (www.nanps.org) for events, seed exchanges, and ways to contact the Missouri Native Plant Society. Also consider the native-plant enthusiasts Wild Ones (www.for-wild.org) for events by a national group as well as by mid-Missouri and St. Louis chapters.

Orchids. The Central Missouri Orchid Society is at cmos.missouri.org. The Orchid Society of Greater St. Louis is at www.osogsl.org. The Orchid Society of Greater Kansas City is www.osgkc.org. The American Orchid Society (www.aos.org) offers links to these and other affiliates in Springfield, southwest Missouri, and Webster Groves.

Rock-garden plants. For the Gateway Chapter of the North American Rock Garden Society, go to www.mobot.org and search "plant societies." The national's Web site is www.nargs.org.

Roses. The Rose Society of Greater St. Louis and the Kansas City Rose Society, among others around the state, are on the American Rose Society's Web site: www.ars.org.

Plant Sources

The independent, local garden centers are on the front lines of home gardening, with staff members and, often these days, horticulturists who know what's right to plant where you live. Garden centers with Web sites are especially helpful, allowing you to "shop" your planting ideas from home. Here are just a few, complete with Web sites. Hundreds more either are members of the Missouri Landscape & Nursery Association (www.mlna.org), the Landscape & Nurserymen's Association of Greater St. Louis (www.stlouislandscape.org), or the Western Nursery and Landscape Association based in Kansas City (www.wnla.org). Start with independent gardens centers, by the way, if you're looking to hire a garden-design professional. Many centers and nurseries have one or more designers on staff.

Ahner's Garden & Gifts, DesPeres: www.ahners.com

Bannister Garden Center, Raymore: www.peonies.net

Bowood Farms, St. Louis: www.bowoodfarms.com

Cottage Garden, Piasa, Illinois, near St. Louis:
www.cottgardens.com

Critical Site Prairie & Wetland Center, Belton: www.critsite.com

Eureka Nursery & Landscaping, Eureka:
www.eurekanursery.com

Fahr Greenhouses, St. Albans: www.fahrgreenhouses.com

Family Tree Nursery, Liberty, Shawnee, and Overland Park:
www.familytreenursery.com

Forrest Keeling Nursery, Elsberry: www.fknursery.com

For the Garden—Haefner's Greenhouse, Oakville:
www.forthegarden.net

Frisella Nursery, Defiance: www.frisellanursery.com

Garden Heights Nursery, Richmond Heights:
www.gardenheights.com

Greenscape Gardens, Ballwin: www.greenscapegardens.net

Hartke Nursery, Olivette: www.hartkenursery.com

Heartland Nursery, Kansas City: www.heartlandnursery.com

Hillermann Nursery & Florist, Washington:
www.hillermann.com

Hummert International, St. Louis: www.hummert.com

Idyllwild Gardens, Savannah: www.idyllwildgardens.com

Longfellow's Garden Center, Centertown;
www.longfellowsgarden.com

Missouri Wildflowers Nursery, Jefferson City:
www.mowildflowers.net

Passiglia's Nursery & Garden Center, Wildwood: www.passiglia.com

Red Cedar Country Gardens, Stilwell, Kansas, near Kansas City:
www.redcedargardens.com

Rolling Ridge Nursery, Webster Groves:
www.rollingridgenursery.com

Sherwoods Forest Nursery & Garden Center, Ballwin:
www.sherwoods-forest.com

Springtime Garden Center, Lee's Summit:
www.springtimegarden.com

Stark Bro's Nurseries & Orchards Co., Louisiana:
www.starkbros.com

Stuckmeyer's Garden Center, Fenton: www.stuckmeyers.com

Suburban Lawn & Garden, Kansas City: www.suburbanlg.com

Sugar Creek Gardens, Kirkwood: www.sugarcreekgardens.com

SummerWinds/Missouri, Ellisvill,e and Lake Saint Louis:
www.summerwindsmo.com

Vintage Hill Farm, Franklin: www.vintagehill.com

Wickman's Garden Village, Springfield: www.wickmans.com

Wine Country Gardens, Defiance: www.winecountrygardens.net

Professional Groups

All-America Selections, an independent, national group, each year announces new garden varieties of flowers, vegetables, and plants that have been tested and proven to be superior for home gardens. It celebrated its seventy-fifth anniversary in 2007. See recent winning plants as well as top selections over the years at www.all-americaselections.org.

All-America Rose Selections. A comparative upstart with a seventieth anniversary in 2008, this nonprofit association of rose growers is dedicated to the introduction and promotion of exceptional roses. See rose winners and other information at www.rose.org.

Horticulture Co-op of Metro St. Louis is an umbrella group for many landscape and gardening individuals and businesses in the St. Louis region, with a terrific Web site aimed, in part, at connecting home gardeners with such services. Go to www.hortco-op.org.

International Society of Arboriculture keeps a list of its certified arborists at the Web address www.isa-arbor.com. To find ones in your area, click on Verify a Certification and then Postal Code to type your zip code. You'll get a rather long list. Be aware that certified arborists who work for local parks departments or city governments generally are not for hire by the home gardener. Look for ones at private firms.

Missouri Landscape and Nursery Association (www.mlna .org) is a statewide not-for-profit organization, says MLNA coordinator MaryAnn Fink, that is "committed to raising the public's horticulture knowledge about successful choices, plants of concern—plants that have 'issues' to be aware of—and featured plants that perform well in Missouri." As a "yellow pages" for the industry, it also features business profiles of its members to help home gardeners find professional help.

Perennial Plant Association (www.perennialplant.org) celebrated its twenty-fifth anniversary in 2007 and is dedicated to helping the home gardener as well as the professional learn more about the best perennials coming to the market. To this end it also chooses a Perennial Plant of the Year by vote of PPA members and by a committee that weighs the choices based on whether a plant is suitable for a wide range of climatic conditions, low maintenance, pest and disease resistant, readily available in the year of release, easily propagated, and ornamentally interesting for multiple seasons.

Prairie Gateway Chapter of the American Society of Landscape Architects (www.pgasla.org) is based in Kansas City but represents landscape architects across Missouri as well as Kansas. Go to the Web site for links to members near you that specialize in such broad garden-design issues as architecture, environmental issues, and historic preservation.

St. Louis Landscape and Nurserymen Association (www.stlouislandscape.org) represents hundreds of area professionals—from greenhouse growers to retail garden centers and landscape designers—all clearly listed under a membership link.

The Western Nursery and Landscape Association (www.wnla.org), as its title implies, represents thousands of horticulture and landscape professionals not only in Missouri and Kansas but also in Iowa, Nebraska, and Oklahoma. Its offices are in St. Joseph.

Publications

Books

Good gardening guides are too numerous to narrow down. Except, that is, for anything by Allan Armitage, the guru of annuals from the University of Georgia's trial gardens (http://ugatrial.hort.uga.edu). And on flowering perennials, Armitage also is somewhat of a national expert. Anything by Michael Dirr is good; he's the dean of woody plants—shrubs and trees. His books are tomes, used as bibles by horticulturists and arborists alike, but also very readable. And any of the American Horticulture Society guides are big, beefy, helpful books for the serious beginner.

As for Missouri books, check out the Missouri Department of Conservation's Nature Shop, at www.mdcnatureshop.com, and look at *Shrubs and Woody Vines of Missouri,* by Don Kurz and artist Paul Nelson; *Trees of Missouri,* also by Kurz; the classic guide by Edgar Denison, *Missouri Wildflowers;* and the new *Central Region Seedling ID Guide for Native Prairie Plants,* for anyone growing natives and who needs to distinguish native seedlings from weeds or other plants.

Monthlies

The *Kansas City Gardener* is a longtime reliable monthly tabloid that's found, free of charge, at garden centers and other sites of botanical interest around the Kansas City region. Newer and also free is *The Gateway Gardener* magazine, the St. Louis region's answer to the Kansas City invention. Go online to www.gatewaygardener.com for more information and locations of every source of this free, gardening-packed publication.

Newspapers

The *Kansas City Star* (www.kansascity.com) often publishes gardening articles, especially in the Saturday House and Home section, with the bonus of an ongoing, online blog for local gardening chat. The *St. Louis Post-Dispatch* (www.stltoday.com) features gardens and gardening issues in its Saturday Lifestyle section.

Seed Sources

Baker Creek Heirloom Seeds, for heirloom vegetable and annual-flower seeds from young collectors who travel the world as well as the state. Go to www.rareseeds.com to browse, to order, or see what's up with seed fairs and festivals at 2278 Baker Creek Road, Mansfield 65704. Call (417) 924-8917. Or go to owner Jere Gettle's new Web site, www.gettle.org.

Hamilton Native Outpost, carrying seeds for native wildflowers as well as for native warm-season grasses, at 16786 Brown Road, Elk Creek 65464. Call (417) 967-2190 or go to www.hamiltonseed.com.

Missouri Wildflowers Nursery, the gold standard against which to judge other such sellers of native Missouri perennials, both seeds and plants. The Web site www.mowildflowers.net features a species list under Plants & Pricing and a good "Growing Information" guide. The mailing address is 9814 Pleasant Hill Road, Jefferson City 65109; phone (573) 496-3492. Mervin Wallace is the guiding force.

Pure Air Native Seed Co., selling large quantities of native warm-season grass and wildflower and legume seeds for wildlife habitats and prairie plantings. The mailing address is 24882 Prairie Grove Trail, Novinger 63559. Call (877) 488-5531 or (660) 488-6849, or go online to www.pureairseed.com.

Sharp Brothers Seed Company, carrying seeds for native grasses and wildflowers, at 396 SW Davis Street, Clinton 64735. Call (800) 451-3779 or go to www.sharpbro.com.

University Resources

Missouri State University and its Department of Fruit Science and State Fruit Experiment Station at Mountain Grove produce a number of online advisories for the home gardener. Go to http://mtngrv.missouristate.edu/MS-18/Index.htm for first-rate information on growing blueberries, strawberries, apples, pears, and other fruit.

MU—University of Missouri Extension is described online as "the local link between the resources of the four University of Missouri campuses and Lincoln University and people throughout the state." That may be an understatement. Extension publications and Web sites offer a monumental amount of home-gardening information. But so do regional offices. Before visiting go to http://extension.missouri.edu and click on County and Regional Extension Centers to find out what's available at the location closest to you.

Perhaps one of the best resources to come under the extension umbrella is the master gardener program. Master gardeners volunteer in community as well as botanical gardens; advise home gardeners on pests, diseases, and best plants for their areas; and conduct fascinating tours of area gardens. Here are just four master gardener Web sites:

- **Greater Kansas City Master Gardeners:** http://extension.missouri.edu/gkcmg
- **Greene County (Springfield) Master Gardeners:** http://extension.missouri.edu/greene/mgg
- **Central Missouri Master Gardeners:** http://extension.missouri.edu/cmregion/mg
- **St. Louis Master Gardeners:** www.stlmg.com

For more information about master gardeners elsewhere in the state, contact Mary Kroening, Missouri state master gardener coordinator in Columbia at (573) 882-9633 or http://extension.missouri.edu/mg.

St. Louis Community College, Meramec Campus, offers the only horticulture-degree program in the St. Louis area. There also is a less arduous certificate option in horticulture offered in conjunction with the Missouri Botanical Garden and including night and weekend classes on such topics as annuals, perennials, trees, shrubs, turfgrasses, and pest identification as well as landscape design and management. See them at www.stlcc.edu/mc/dept/hortcltr. The Meramec campus, at 11333 Big Bend Boulevard in Kirkwood, is home to a significant early-spring event every other year, called the St. Louis Garden Symposium, open to amateurs and professionals alike. It alternates years with a similar program across the state, called the Kansas City Garden Symposium, presented by Friends of Powell Gardens. Closer to the times of each city's events, go to Web sites of either sponsoring group—in St. Louis, the Horticulture Co-op of Metropolitan St. Louis, at www.hortco-op.org; in Kansas City, at www.powell gardens.org.

Truman State University and its campus, at 100 East Normal Street, in Kirksville 63501, near the Iowa border, includes a four-hundred-acre University Farm that's open to the public by appointment. Besides agriculture operations, visitors see such home-gardening elements as newly planted apple trees, a greenhouse, and a vineyard testing French-hybrid grapes for growing in northern Missouri soils and weather. Bill Kuntz is the farm manager; contact him at (660) 785-7477, or visit www.truman.edu and search "farm."

Glossary

acidic soil: Soil with a pH value of less than 7. Vegetables and most ornamentals do best in slightly acidic soil with a pH range of 6 to 7.

alkaline soil: Soil with a pH of more than 7. Ground limestone products often are used to increase pH; aluminum sulfate and sulfur are generally used to decrease pH.

annual: A plant that germinates, matures, sets seed, and dies in one growing season.

bacteria: Organisms in soil—some are pathogens, but most are decomposers that break down organic matter and make it useful to plants.

biennial: A plant that flowers and dies in its second growing season.

clay soil: Soil made of fine mineral particles, plus sand and silt, with a dense structure that means it drains slowly but also holds on to nutrients.

chemical fertilizer: Chemical, or inorganic, fertilizers are made from nonliving materials and often through chemical reactions.

chlorosis: Yellowing of leaves from lack of chlorophyll—possibly from nutrient deficiencies or other problems in the soil. A soil test is recommended.

climate: Elements of weather in a specific region, including rainfall, snowfall, temperature, humidity, frost, and ice storms, among others.

cold frame: A glass-covered box or frame that works outdoors as a small greenhouse, protecting plants and seedlings from frost.

cold-hardiness zones: Several sets of zones, researched and drawn on U.S. maps—primarily by the USDA, but also separately by the Arbor Day Foundation and by the American Horticulture Society—to help determine what perennial and woody plants survive winters in a region.

compost: An organic material formed by decomposed plants and other organic matter. It is made in the home garden from one part grass clippings—or "green" waste—to two parts dried leaves, or "brown" plant material.

cool-season grass: A perennial turf, such as Kentucky bluegrass or turf-type tall fescue, that thrives at temperatures of around 60 to 75 degrees Fahrenheit.

crown: A plant's part—at soil level—where roots and stems join and from which new shoots grow.

cultivar: A named variety of plant, with specific characteristics.

deadheading: The removal of a plant's spent blooms to stimulate new flower growth.

deciduous: Any tree or shrub that loses its leaves in winter and renews them in spring.

determinant: Type of tomato plant that's bushy, relatively short, and good for growing in pots.

division: Increasing perennials by dividing them into pieces, each with a root system and shoots.

drip irrigation: A watering method that uses hoses with tiny outlets called emitters that target water directly to roots.

freeze and thaw: Cycles in winter of cold temperatures that freeze water in soil, alternating with warmer temperatures that thaw the water (see "heaving").

fungi: Parasitic plants that lack chlorophyll and leaves and that reproduce by spores. Both beneficial and disease-causing types occur, in the soil and on leaf surfaces.

growing season: The weeks between the last frost of spring and the first of fall.

grub: Larva stage of an insect—such as the Japanese beetle—during its life cycle.

half-hardy annual: A plant that will survive some cold but will not overwinter outdoors.

half-hardy perennial: A perennial that needs some protection (such as mulch) from winter cold.

hardening off: The process of acclimatizing plants grown indoors to outdoor temperatures, sun, and the drying effects of wind.

hardy annual: A plant—such as the pansy—that may be planted in fall and well mulched for spring flowers.

hardy perennials: Plants that can survive very cold winters with little or no protection.

heaving: An upward movement of plants and roots, exposing them in winter after freezing and thawing of soil.

herbaceous perennial: A plant with stems, leaves, and flowers that die back to the ground in fall. New growth emerges again in spring.

herbicide: A chemical that kills vegetation.

horticultural oil: A substance, often organic, that is sprayed on plants to suffocate insects at various stages, especially eggs of scale, aphids, whiteflies, and mealybugs.

hybrid: A plant that is the result of intentional breeding, or crossing, of two plants with different genetic material. Seeds from hybrids will not breed true.

indeterminant: Tallest type of tomato plant that grows, flowers, and fruits until frost.

insecticidal soap: A substance generally approved for organic use and made from potassium salts of fatty acids used to disrupt cell-membrane structure of soft-bodied insects.

insecticide: A substance that kills insects and, often, is made from inorganic chemicals.

integrated pest management (IPM): A commonsense, earth-friendly method of dealing with plant disease and pest damage by focusing on the least toxic approaches.

invasive plants: Plants not native to the United States that crowd out native species and cause environmental and economic harm.

loam: A soil type with a balance of sand, silt, and clay; good texture; good drainage; and proper amounts of moisture and air.

macronutrients: Nitrogen (N), phosphorus (P), and potassium (K)—three of several most-important elements used by plants in large amounts for growth.

manure: Animal droppings often used as soil amendments after aging or composting.

microclimate: Pockets of warmer or colder air and soil within a hardiness zone.

micronutrients: Elements—such as iron, zinc, and manganese—found in small, or trace, amounts in soil but important for proper plant growth.

mulch: Compost, aged manure, wood chips, pine needles, or other materials applied to the soil surface to help conserve water and suppress weeds.

mycorrhizae: Soil fungi that share minerals with plant roots and with their fine extensions—called root hairs—in a helpful symbiotic relationship.

native plant: A plant that's grown in North America since before European settlement.

organic fertilizer: Fertilizer made from natural ingredients, such as the by-products of plants and animals and naturally occurring minerals.

pathogen: A disease-causing agent such as a bacterium, virus, or fungus.

peat moss: An organic, somewhat acidic soil additive harvested from bogs. It helps keep potting mixes from compacting but has little nutritional value for plants.

perennial: Any plant that comes back year after year.

rhizomes: Stems that travel under the surface of the soil.

sandy soils: Soils predominantly made of large mineral particles.

scapes: Leafless flower stems; daylily blossoms, for example, grow on scapes.

self-sower: An annual or biennial that deposits seeds, germinating in the garden the following year.

silt: Soil made of medium-size mineral particles.

silty soils: Soils made predominantly of medium-size mineral particles.

soaker hose: An irrigation hose that "sweats" water along its entire length.

sod: Fully grown turf that is cut in strips to be laid on prepared soil for instant lawn.

soil amendments: Materials such as aged animal manure, compost, and slow-release organic fertilizers added to soil to improve drainage, aeration, and moisture conditions.

soil test: An analysis of a soil's pH, nutrient content, structure, and other factors important to plant growth.

soil texture: The particular blend of a soil, depending on the amounts of sand, silt, and clay that are present.

subsoil: The layer beneath topsoil in which there are few nutrients and less root growth.

tender perennial: A perennial that won't survive winter unless lifted and stored in frost-free conditions for replanting in spring.

tilth: A fine, crumbly surface layer of cultivated soil.

topdressing: Compost, fertilizer, or aged manure placed on the soil surface around plants to replenish nutrients.

topping: The practice—often opposed by arborists—of cutting tree branches to stubs that, in turn, may stress the trees and open them to disease and decay.

topsoil: The first layer of soil, from which plant roots get most of their water and nutrients.

transition zone: The transition between northern and southern regions for turfgrass, where neither warm-season nor cool-season grasses are completely comfortable.

tropical: A plant that's native to the tropics and is often grown as a houseplant and, increasingly, is grown in gardens or containers outdoors, to be overwintered indoors.

warm-season grass: Turf-grass types growing optimally in temperatures of 80 to 95 degrees. Zoysia, Bermuda grass, even buffalo grass do best in such heat.

woody perennial: A plant with woody, stiff stems that do not die back to the crown.

xeriscaping: Landscaping that uses native and drought-tolerant plants.

Index

feather reed grass, 106–7
ferns, 93
fertilizers,
    chemical, 101
    organic, 70–71, 101–2, 139–40
fescue, turf-type, 132–33
Fink, MaryAnn, 25–26
fire blight, 157
firecracker plant, 61
flowering dogwood, 115
foamflower, 87
Forest Park, 165
forsythia, 128
fox sedge, 94
fragrant sumac, 90
freeze-thaw, 29, 45
Fresenburg, Brad, 131, 134
frost hardiness, 21
fruit, 81–84
    disease resistance, 83
    suggested varieties, 81–84
    tree care, 82
    when to plant, 83

garden centers and nurseries,
    176–78
garden clubs, 170
garden designers, 86–87, 126–28,
    177–80
gardening resources Web sites,
    171–73
garden tours, 167, 170, 183
garlic, 75
Garner, Cindy, 118–19
Gateway Gardener magazine, 181
geranium, 56–57, 107
Gettle, Jere, 52–54, 76–80
ginkgo, 121
glory-of-the-snow, 113

gooseneck loosestrife, 151
grasses
    native, 90–91
    nonnative, 106–7
gray-head coneflower, 90
Great Perennial Divide, 102
greenhouses, 31–33
Grim, Trish, 67, 76–80
growing seasons, 20–33
Grow Native!, 85, 89, 95, 171
Guinan, Pat, 20–21, 27–30, 34, 36

hardening off, 21
hardiness zones, cold, 22–25
Heartland Tree Alliance, 171
heat-tolerant plants, 30–31, 114
heat zones, 30
heirloom garden, 79
Heirloom Seed Festival, 52, 167
heirloom seeds, 51–53, 79, 167
herbicide, 147
herbs, 68–76, 175–76
herb societies, 73, 76, 175
Hermann, Jan, 68
Hinkle, Lynn, 42
hollyhock, 53
Horticulture Co-op of Metro St.
    Louis, 179
hosta, 100, 107–8, 176
    Hosta of the Year, 108
hummingbird, plants for, 49,
    61, 110
Hutson, June, 14, 28
hydrangeas, 129

impatiens, 57
insect control, 71–72
insecticidal soap, 153–55
insects, 152–55

organic matter, 5, 70–71
ostrich fern, 93
Overland Park Arboretum and
    Botanical Gardens, 163
ozarksgardens.com, 59, 173

pansy, 57–58
parsley, 74
peach, 82–83
peony, 108–9
pepper, 78
perennials, 97–114
    bulbs as, 112–14
    deer and rabbit resistant, 112
    defined, 97
    dividing, 102
    fertilizers, 101–2, 113
    fragrant, 98, 100, 108
    organic gardening of, 70–72,
        101–2
    planning by theme, 98–100
    suggested varieties, 103–12
    sun versus shade, 100–101
    watering, 101–2
Perennial Plant Association, 180
Perennial Plant of the Year, 104,
    106–7, 109
pests and diseases, 144–59
    animal pests, 155–56
    beneficial insects, 152
    biological controls, 71–72
    common diseases, 151–52,
        156–58
    insect pests, 152–55
    weeding, 145
petunia, 58
pH, 9–13, 71
phosphorus, 13
plant festivals, 167

plant sales, 76, 170, 174–75
plant societies, 174–76
Plants of Merit, 55–56, 60,
    90–91, 93–94, 103–4, 107–9,
    113, 127–29, 140, 151, 163
potassium, 13
Potter, Dennis, 2
powdery mildew, 39
Powell Gardens, 65, 84, 88, 95,
    161, 163–64, 173
prairie blazing star, 91
prairie dropseed, 91
prairie onion, 114
precipitation, 34–36
public gardens, 160–68
purple beardtongue, 91
purple coneflower, 87, 92, 97, 98
purple loosestrife, 149–50

Quinn, James, 8–9, 12–13

rabbits, 155–56
rain gardens, 42–44, 85, 92
raised beds, 68–70
redbud, 124
redtwig dogwood, 130
ribbon grass, 151
river birch, 124–25
Roberts, Paul, 131–39
Robinson, George R., 137
rock garden societies, 176
Rodgers, Rhonda, 79
rosarians, consulting, 112
rosemary, 74
rose rosette disease, 158
roses, 111–12, 157, 176, 179
royal fern, 93
rust, 158